GOING
to the
MOUNTAIN

GOING to the MOUNTAIN

*Lessons for
Life's Journey*

ROSALIE T. TURNER

© 2002 by Rosalie T. Turner. All rights reserved

Printed in the United States of America

Pleasant Word (a division of WinePress Publishing, PO Box 428, Enumclaw, WA 98022) functions only as book publisher. As such, the ultimate design, content, editorial accuracy, and views expressed or implied in this work are those of the author.

No part of this publication may be reproduced, stored in a retrieval system or transmitted in any way by any means—electronic, mechanical, photocopy, recording or otherwise—without the prior permission of the copyright holder, except as provided by USA copyright law.

Unless otherwise noted, all Scriptures are taken from *Good News Bible—The Bible In Today's English Version—* American Bible Society. New York, 1966, 1971, 1976. Used by permission.

Scripture references marked KJV are taken from the King James Version of the Bible.

ISBN 1-4141-0686-6
Library of Congress Catalog Card Number: 2001093865

To Ed and Merle Ridout

who understand and live the real meaning of ministry

In memory of

Ann Logan Birckhead,

whose life was a ministry to many

Acknowledgment

I gratefully acknowledge the use of the original oil painting by New Mexico artist, Bill Curry, for use on the cover of this book. His work may be viewed at the Sundowner Gallery in Tucumcari, New Mexico.

The snow-capped mountain in the painting is Wheeler Peak, New Mexico's tallest mountain. Two weeks before Terry was diagnosed with leukemia, the family was vacationing in the shadow of this mountain, and Terry and his dad had a special overnight camping trip, hiking to its upper reaches.

Contents

Prologue ix
Chapter 1   Take One Day at a Time 17
Chapter 2   Let It All Out 29
Chapter 3   Give Thanks . . . in Everything? 37
Chapter 4   Reach Out and Touch Someone 49
Chapter 5   The Best Day of My Life 63
Chapter 6   There's No Such Thing as Pixie Dust 71
Chapter 7   Walking through the Valley 83
Chapter 8   ". . . And the Other Is Wings" 99
Chapter 9   Like a Rock 111
Chapter 10 "O for a Thousand Tongues to Sing" 123
Epilogue 133
Endnotes 137

Prologue

As I drove up the mountain in northern New Mexico last spring, I could feel my spirits lifting as I wound my way up the road, higher and higher. The road was clear, but a pure, pristine white snow covered the ground. As far as the eye could see was the natural beauty of the mountains, one ridge after another, the bold green of pine and fir standing between a stark white blanket of snow and the deep blue of a New Mexico sky. It was an affirmation of the unfettered loveliness of God's world. I was alone on the road. There was no one or nothing to distract me from savoring every nuance of the beauty before me. I was so moved by the scene I found my eyes filling with tears. I pulled the car over to a stop and felt a strong urge to praise the Lord who made all this. It was unbelievably beautiful. It was incredibly majestic. It was . . . a true worship experience.

I think that is one of the reasons God made mountains. They bring us up, out of ourselves, and set us on a higher plane, a little closer to Him. They provide for us a place where we can come away from the every day world; a place where it's easier to find silence so we might better hear that special voice with which He speaks to us.

God has used mountains from the very beginning of time. The Scriptures are full of them, from Mt. Sinai to Mount Carmel to the Mount of Olives.

Beginning in Genesis we find references to the importance of mountains. Genesis 8 tells of the end of Noah's dealing with the flood. "On the seventeenth day of the seventh month the boat came to rest on a mountain in the Ararat range. The water kept going down and on the first day of the tenth month the tops of the mountains appeared" (Genesis 8:4,5). I can only imagine how grateful Noah and his family felt for mountains at that point in time!

Also in Genesis we see a completely different perspective of a mountain. It becomes a place of testing for Abraham when God commanded him to sacrifice his precious son, Isaac. "'Take your son,' God said, 'your only son, Isaac, whom you love so much, and go to the land of Moriah. There on a mountain that I will show you, offer him as a sacrifice to me'" (Genesis 22:2). Rather than lifting him up, that journey of each step up the mountain must have been a terrible one for Abraham. It was because Abraham knew that God was with him every step, that he was able to make that climb. He was able to build the altar and prepare to sacrifice Isaac. At the eleventh hour, he was able to hear the angel when he spoke and told Abraham not to sacrifice the boy. Abraham then saw a ram nearby to use for the sacrifice instead of his beloved son, so he named the place "The Lord Provides." Genesis 22:14 says, "And even today people say, 'On the Lord's mountain he provides.'"

One of the most vivid Old Testament images of a mountain comes with the story of Moses as he goes up Mt. Sinai

Prologue

to meet with God. I believe God sent Moses to Mt. Sinai for the same reason He wants us to go the mountains. We know that God doesn't live only on the top of a mountain, but we learn that to be able to "talk" to God we need to go to a special place. That place might be an actual physical place, or it might be simply a special place inside us, a place where we can tune out the world and tune in to God. In order to discern our Father, we need such a place, a place that lifts us out of the everyday in the way that going up a mountain does.

Immediately after His baptism and before He could start his ministry, Jesus went to the mountain. It is there He deals with His temptation. "Then the Devil took Jesus to a very high mountain and showed Him all the kingdoms of the world in all their greatness. 'All this I will give You,' the Devil said, 'if You will kneel down and worship me'" (Matthew 4:8). Jesus came down from the mountain, strong and sure in His faith and purpose, and began to gather His disciples.

His ministry then began and soon large crowds are following Him. We see, over and over, that Jesus goes up a hill or mountain to set apart a special time. This special time might be for teaching others or it might be for Him to communicate alone with His Father. Matthew 5:1,2 tells us, "Jesus saw the crowds and went up a hill, where He sat down. His disciples gathered around Him, and He began to teach them."

There are several references to the fact that when Jesus wanted to be in deep and close prayer with his Father, He would go up a hill or mountainside. "Jesus left there and went along by Lake Galilee. He climbed a hill and sat down" (Matthew 15:29). "Then Jesus went up a hill and called to Himself the men He wanted" (Mark 3:13). "Jesus spent those days teaching in the Temple, and when evening came, He would go out and spend the night on the Mount of Olives" (Luke 21:37). "Jesus went up a hill and sat down with His disciples" (John 6:3). What followed was the feeding of the five thousand.

The image of mountains continues in Jesus' ministry. He is on the Mount of Olives when He tells the disciples about what is to come. He, with Peter, James, and John, are up on a mountain when the Transfiguration takes place. "Six days later Jesus took with Him Peter and the brothers James and John and led them up a high mountain where they were alone. As they looked on, a change came over Jesus: His face was shining like the sun, and His clothes were dazzling white . . . and a voice from the cloud said, 'This is My own dear Son with whom I am pleased: listen to Him!'" (Matthew 17:1,2,5). After the final Passover meal with His disciples, they go again to the Mount of Olives.

Over and over in Scriptures we see that mountains were places for God to reach out to His people.

I have a place like that where I go in the mountains. It is a special place, a sacred and holy place, a place of peace. It is a place where I can feel God's presence and hear His voice. It is a high place at a curve in the road. I can pull off the dirt road and look out over the valley. There are mountains of green on either side, and far off in the distance rise the majestic peaks of the tallest mountain in New Mexico. The valley is a gentle quilt below sprinkled with ranches, an ambling stream, and gatherings of scrub oak, aspen, and juniper. Like Jesus did, I go there to talk with the Father, or to listen for what He might say to me. It's easier for me to hear Him up there. I see His works in every direction. The stillness and the clean fresh air somehow make it easier for me to connect with Him. Of course, I don't hear His actual

Prologue

voice, but there is a place within me that becomes peaceful and seems to nudge my thoughts in the ways He would have them go.

I have taken several people there. Even though it is my special place, it is something I want to share with people I care about. I don't take everyone there, but if someone visiting us is hurting in some way, I am sure to take him or her there. It is a place of peace and it can be a place of healing. The way the valley stretches out below in such beautiful order makes me feel that I am sitting in the heel of God's hand looking across his palm and fingers outstretched. If I am in God's hand, I am safe. I am comforted. If God is for me, who can be against me? (Romans 8:31).

I carry this special place with me in my heart and in my mind's eye. Wherever I am I can picture it. I can almost feel the mountain breeze in my hair, almost smell the pines, almost see the wild purple iris seeming to dance to the music of a wind that feels like the caress of a gentle hand.

I believe that there is a place like that for each of us, and that we need to find that place. We need to come to that place because it is where we can be most alive, be the best of ourselves, be the closest to the living Lord. It is a place we can carry within us as we travel on through life, and it will strengthen us in that journey. The Spanish have a word for such a place, "querencia." It can't really be translated, but it means a place that is ours; it is a place where we feel that we belong.

I think that for Jesus, His "querencia" was on a mountain. I think that in the act of climbing, He could feel Himself drawing closer to His Father. In doing this, Jesus was showing us that while God is always there for us, a response on our part is required. We need to go to the Father. We need to climb the mountain to get closer to Him, just as Jesus did.

Mountains are referred to throughout the Bible. They are places to which people flee. They are the places to which people journey. They are places where altars are built, and where people are buried. Mountains are the places where God appeared. They are places of battle, and they are places of glory. Whatever else they are, they are God's place, a unique and powerful image for us.

When we talk about a special experience in our walk of faith, we often speak of a "mountaintop experience." I've had such experiences, and you probably have had them too. Often they happen when we are on a retreat or have in some way separated ourselves from our everyday world.

I can remember a few such experiences from my high school years. It was during these mountaintop experiences that I knew there was a living Lord who cared about me. I gleaned this knowledge from those experiences and it gave me strength and comfort when I went back to my world. I had a home life in turmoil, a world where my parents, while meaning to be good parents, were so caught up in their own difficulties they could not get past their own anger and unhappiness. I love the understanding that I got from the story of Ruth, who went as a poor widow to her beloved mother-in-law's land (Ruth 1:1–2:14). In reading about her gleaning from the fields belonging to Boaz, I could visualize how the fields were left after the first harvesting so the widows and orphans could gather grain for themselves. It's like being able to take precious nuggets that we need for our very nourishment. That was how I felt about what I learned from my mountaintop experiences. That knowledge was a precious nugget of nourishment that fed and sustained me.

I still have a letter I wrote to myself on a retreat thirty-five years ago when my husband and I were in our early

Prologue

years of our marriage. We were counselors for a youth group at our church in California. It had been a wonderful week of study, fun, and spiritual growth. At the last campfire the minister told each of us to return in silence to our cabins and write a letter to ourselves about our experience there. Over the years I have reread that letter, and I am transported back to that time.

It was one of the highest mountaintops I've ever been on. God is Love, and Love was what filled me. I had married a wonderful man whom I dearly loved and who loved me. We were happy in our home and in our activities. We loved our church and had become very close to the young people. We were expecting our first-born child in a few months and I felt blessed beyond measure.

I am still married to that same wonderful man, and I love him now more dearly than I did then, just as he loves me. We have continued to be happy in our homes and activities, even though my husband's career has moved us sixteen times in those thirty-eight years. We've loved our churches and been close to young people in other youth groups, and people of all ages in our different churches. We've had two more sons who have been a blessing to us.

And our first-born whom we were expecting? We had a beautiful baby boy, blond hair with blue eyes. He was bright and fun and healthy . . . until . . . until a fateful, terrible day when he was eight years old and we learned he had a rare form of leukemia and would not live much longer. We buried him a month after his tenth birthday. Heartbroken? Yes. Devastated? Yes. We wondered if we could ever get on with life again . . . and yet. . . .

Yet even now, so many years later, I would still say that I have been blessed beyond measure. I had always said that I could not bear it if anything ever happened to my children, but something did happen, and I did bear it. I still know the living Lord who loves me. I marvel at God's giving me that gift, the gift of dealing with one of life's most difficult struggles, and yet still believing in mountaintops. How could I still feel blessed, I sometimes wonder?

I have come to realize over the years that God has taught me certain lessons; lessons that I need to get through life's journey successfully. This book is a sharing of those lessons, with the hope and prayer that it might make someone else's journey a little easier.

The other thing I have learned is that we cannot have mountains without valleys. It is the valleys that define the mountains. We could never understand the height of a mountain unless we start from the valley and work our way up. I believe that God gave us a wonderful image by which we can understand life when he gave us mountains and valleys.

I believe that God wants us to have mountaintop experiences; He wants us to come to the mountains to meet Him. How do we learn to do that? What are the things we need to do in life that make mountaintops possible?

In keeping with that idea, I have written this book. Introducing each chapter is a "valley" section, an excerpt from my journal as I dealt with our son's illness, death and our life after his death. The chapters however, are the "mountains," the lessons I have learned that make life successful, and that make me want to worship a God who has made the beauty of my "querencia" in the mountains. I share my learning about a Lord who helps me understand my life is full and richly abundant, a Father who loves me and helps me love others, and a Friend who is with me always.

Discussion questions follow each chapter if the book is used as a small group study book, or simply for the reader to consider.

Take One Day at a Time

THE VALLEY

I'm afraid, Lord. I'm not sure I even know what to be afraid of, but the fear is there, overwhelming me. The doctor told us, "a blood infection. . . . yes, it could be leukemia . . . St. Jude Children's Research Hospital . . . fly there immediately." How could this happen to US? I wear my sunglasses so no one can see the fear and anguish in my eyes.

Finally at St. Jude's, they say it is leukemia, a rare kind. If we are lucky our first-born son might live a year. I don't think I can grasp that yet, Lord. It's too much to bear. There are other concerns to ward off dealing with that, like will he make it through tonight? Will the hemorrhaging stop? How do we tell the grandparents? How can we keep our younger son's life as normal as possible?

I guess our first lesson is being learned. They told us, "Take one day at a time." We can't deal with the "why?" so we have to turn to the things we can do, even if it is only reading to our *boy, lying pale in the hospital bed. We must turn to the things we CAN do. Please help us!*

THE MOUNTAIN

Remembering that first day, I can recall the very moment the doctors told us it was leukemia. Even after all these years it is as vivid to me as it was then.

After the examinations, blood tests, and the spinal tap at St. Jude's, they settled our son Terry in a hospital bed and told us they would come back for my husband and me in about ten minutes to go over the diagnosis.

Those ten minutes lengthened into a half hour, and that half hour stretched into an hour. We began to hope again, to think that perhaps they couldn't find any traces of the leukemia after all. Finally, when they did take us into a consultation room, they said the delay was because they wanted to be in complete agreement about the diagnosis since it was a rare kind of leukemia with a very poor prognosis.

We broke down then, sobbing, groping for each other's hand, completely and utterly devastated. The doctors sat quietly waiting. We wept on. It was too much. Too much!

Finally, in a kind of furious desperation, I asked, "But what do we do now? What CAN we do?"

"Ah," said Dr. Simone, smiling at us, "That's what I've been waiting for."

We looked at him expectantly.

"You can rail against this and ask yourselves 'why' forever, but it won't help. You'll never get to the answer. You'll just be spinning your wheels. The only way to handle this is one day at a time. There are things you can do, one day at a time. Now, here's what we can do." He outlined a program of chemotherapy and radiation that might lead to the remission of Terry's leukemia.

"Take one day at a time." Difficult advice to heed? Oh, yes, especially at first.

At first we simply struggled and struggled against it. We tried staying in control of our lives, planning how the weeks and months ahead should progress. It was like taking children's blocks and trying to build a tower, stacking layer upon layer. Suddenly, something would happen—fevers, no response to chemotherapy, our overwhelming sense of despair—and it was as if someone had swiped at our tower knocking it to pieces.

When we tried looking beyond the present terrors to consider the long-term future, we could only see a dark and terrifying void because of Terry's poor prognosis.

I felt so angry with the doctors for telling us to take one day at a time. It was easy for them to say because Terry wasn't their son. It wasn't their family who looked at each other with eyes spilling pain and anguish. Their sons had futures. Our son, our bright and beautiful son, what could we promise him now?

Slowly, very, very slowly, I faced the truth we all know deep inside. Really, there is not much we can promise our children. We can't promise them a life without problems. We can't promise them the perfect mate or the most rewarding career. We can't even promise them that we'll always be there for them. I came to realize that the only thing I could promise Terry was a loving God who would always be with him. When I finally realized that, I realized that a loving God was all I could ever have promised him, even if he had never become ill. That helped me to begin the process of letting go of future dreams and plans and start dealing with the todays.

I believe that somehow we have to develop a mindset or a habit, of taking one day at a time until it becomes automatic for us. I didn't want to have to learn that lesson. I had always been the kind of person who loved planning things, who enjoyed the expectation of things to come, but I felt God working on my heart, telling me that the best way to make this journey would be to do it one day at a time.

I remember one particular morning the first week we were at St. Jude. We still did not know if Terry would live through the week because he was so ill. I was back at the coffee shop in the motel trying to get a cup of coffee to slide past the constant lump in my throat. I noticed a family nearby with a boy a few years younger than Terry. They were laughing together, and the boy was skipping around the table, eyes sparkling with mischief and life. He was dressed in a T-shirt and shorts and was wearing one of those toy hardhats that looked like the hardhat a baseball player wears for batting. They were obviously a happy, healthy family on vacation, enjoying life to the fullest. Comparing their situation to ours was heartbreaking. I was so furious that God would allow them to be there in front of me that I couldn't even stay to finish my coffee.

Later that day at the hospital, I went with Terry to the X-ray and radiation area. There, waiting, sat the family I had seen that morning. The young boy was giving his mother his hat to hold, and as he took it off I saw that his head was completely bald. He had lost all his hair from his cancer treatments. This was not the happy, healthy, vacationing family I had thought they were, but instead they were a family like us, enduring the unendurable.

I felt as though someone had knocked the air out of me. Here was a family like us, and yet, they had joy. In the midst of despair, there could be moments of joy. What a powerful message! I sensed a glimmering in that lesson of what it meant to take one day at a time, moment by moment. What I know now is that this is a good lesson for us at any point in our lives, whether in the middle of bad times or good times or in-between times.

We've all heard the cliché that today is all we have, and we understand the truth of that. We've all probably known or read of people who, upon discovering they have a terminal illness, tell of how they have started savoring the moments of each day. One support group is even called Make Today Count. Why is it we have to wait for that kind of sentencing before we can "stop to smell the roses" along the way? Is that simply human nature?

We hurriedly rush ahead, intent on our busy-ness. We need to accomplish this, get that done, go there, and be here. It happens to all of us it seems, and in present-day America, it has become a way of life.

One of my husband's fondest memories of his childhood is visiting his grandparents' home during summer vacation. He has told me of evenings with his family sitting out on the front porch, visiting with neighbors who passed by, sharing stories, or just watching the stars fill the summer sky. I've seen pictures of that old house with the wooden porch swing, and I can picture those evenings. I recently read that they don't build porches like that anymore because people aren't taking the time to sit on them after supper—or any time. I think that's sad. That old custom was a way of taking time for today, of taking just one day at a time. It was a time for savoring the moment.

That slow easy way of life seems to be gone forever from our country. Even with our hectic pace, I think it is still possible to follow the philosophy of taking one day at a time. It just won't be as easy. We'll have to work at it a little harder, mold it a little more firmly into our lifestyle.

Perhaps one way to accomplish that is to do what a friend of mine does. Every day when she first wakes up, she says these words of praise, "This is the day that the Lord has made. Let us rejoice and be glad in it" (Psalm 118:24 KJV).

"THIS is the day . . ." is the emphasis I need, while placing the day within the framework of God's love. If I can get that idea fixed firmly in my mind as I begin the day it will be easier to get into the mindset of taking one day at a time; taking today and making it all it can be.

There are many places in Scripture where we can find support for the idea of taking one day at a time, but perhaps none is more emphatic than in the Lord's Prayer. This prayer, which is such a dynamic summary of Christian theology, states, "Give us THIS day our daily bread." It is THIS day we are to ask for, not tomorrow. Today is the emphasis that Christ Himself teaches us. Problems can come when we spend our todays dreaming only of what tomorrow might bring or stewing over what yesterday brought.

I know a man who has spent years of his life angry and frustrated over a bad relationship from his past. One day, as we talked, he began to recount specific details of a supposed injustice he thought this person had done to him. As he recited detail after detail, his face got redder and redder and he became more and more angry.

Finally, I put my hand on his arm. "That was thirty years ago," I said. "Thirty years! What can that possibly have to do with right now? That person isn't even alive any longer. What happened so long ago is just extra baggage for you. Why not just drop it now and leave it behind where it belongs?"

At a Bible study recently, our gifted leader suggested that we each spend a few hours alone with a pad and pencil and go with God to clear out some of that debris we all have accumulated. She said we should think of it as an old smelly gym locker. There might be things in there that we have confessed, but never really repented of. There might be hurts and pains we have never let go of, things we have never really forgiven, times when we have been separated from God. Until we clear out all that old stuff, like dirty socks from a gym locker, we can never be all that God means for us to be. We need to get rid of those "dirty socks" before we really can value and enjoy our moments.

Sometimes though, what we carry from the past might not be negative memories, but cherished ones. If we hang on to them in such a way that there is no room to appreciate what is happening today, then that can be just as destructive as if there were negative memories.

There was a woman who had been successful in her career, enjoying the benefits of a financially secure marriage as yet unenriched and unencumbered by the responsibility of children. Later, staying home as the mother of young children, she began to feel cheated. She remembered the stimulation of a day out in the business world, of feeling successful about goals set and reached. She remembered a time when she was appreciated and valued for a job well done.

The more her mind would cling to those memories the more the small irritations of the days at home with her two young children loomed as major annoyances. She became unable to appreciate the day-to-day joys of being with her children, seeing them grow and change. Finally, she made the decision to return to work.

If she had been able to develop the philosophy of taking one day at a time, at least she would have had another option. Perhaps then she could have looked at the small daily irritations as just that, not as the major hurdles of constant stress, which they became for her.

What of looking ahead? How can that steal from my todays? If I fill my mind with dreams of what might be or worries of the same then I have no room for enjoying what I have right now. If I am always looking ahead I will tend to miss the smaller moments of life, and often these are the most precious—a beautiful sunset, a song that touches me deeply, a friend's smile, a child putting his hand trustingly in mine. Sometimes I am so filled with an anxiousness to get on with life, to see what is going to happen, that I never see what is happening now. If that is the way I live, I lose those moments that I can never get back.

How many times have we worried about something that might happen? We imagine and prepare ourselves for various scenarios, dreading the worst and feeling all the emotions of going through that scenario. Then, when it doesn't happen we feel a sense of relief. In the meantime, we have wasted all that time and emotional energy for nothing and by being caught up in that future concern, we have missed the moments of that day.

When I think about it, I realize that all my life God has been trying to teach me to take one day at a time, but I seem to keep resisting the lesson. Fortunately, He finds yet another way to show me.

I can remember so vividly the family trips driving cross-country during my childhood. It was in the days before interstate highways, and the routes were so much more interesting than the sameness of interstate travel today.

I can remember passing through one part of the country and thinking, "This is so beautiful. I wish we could just stay here." We'd keep on going though and when we'd get to another area I'd think, "I'm so glad we didn't stay back there because THIS is so beautiful!" Whichever section of the country we went through had its own beauty for me to discover, its own uniqueness which I could enjoy in that "today" because we hadn't stayed in the "yesterday" of places already past.

Realizing the value of living one day at a time, of living in the moment, is only the first step. The second step is finding those things that help us automatically appreciate the moment. For each of us there will be certain "triggers" that remind us; triggers that put us back on track.

One way of developing an appreciation for one day at a time, I've found, is having a regular, daily prayer and meditation time. Our Scriptures teach us that God wants us to value and live in our todays. Having a regular time to be in the Word, being quiet so I can hear God's voice in my life, I find that I can more easily align myself with what He wants me to do. I believe that one thing He wants me to do is to cherish the moment.

Whether I am busy looking forward to something with eager anticipation or dreading the future, it can rob me of my todays. Fear and worry about tomorrow are common in life, but if I can feel God's presence in my today, I am less likely to be overwhelmed. There is a poster that says, "There is nothing that can happen today that God and I can't handle."

The best thing I have learned about one-day-at-a-time is that God promises to be with us in that one day. No matter what happens to us in life, if we learn to break it down into dealing with it just for today and knowing that God is with us in that today, there is nothing that can defeat us. What a powerful thought!

Another way to help us live one day at a time is to be orderly with our time even though this seems to be almost impossible in the world today. The days rush into each other until time is a blur. This, I believe, is why we have the idea of "Sabbath." We all need a time of rest, of restoration, a time to take a deep breath and pause for awhile.

I like to think of Sabbath not as a specific day, but as a state of mind. If we each took time for Sabbath it would be easier for us to focus on the day, moment by moment. In order to celebrate Sabbath, I think, we must each find what our personal Sabbath might be. Where do we find our own rest? Is it in family activity, or gardening, or going for a long walk? Could it be in reading or Bible study or listening to music? God made each of us to be different and unique so our Sabbath expressions will be different and unique. Whatever it might be, keeping the Sabbath is necessary to us. It will be that which restores us, which can bring a sense of peace to our soul. To have time for a Sabbath we will have to reprioritize. The work of prioritizing will help us put our activities and moments into perspective. When these moments are in perspective, we can more easily live one day at a time.

One-day-at-a-time has been a difficult lesson for me to learn, but it has been worth it when I follow that lesson. I think it is true for all of us that we can more easily get through the bad times when we handle them one day at a time. We can savor the good times when we handle them one day at a time. We can rest and use our in-between times for study and growth, healing and restoring.

A guest speaker at our Sunday school class shared this with us. It is simply attributed to Helen Mallicoat.

I was regretting the past and fearing the future. Suddenly my Lord was speaking.

"My name is I Am." He paused; I waited. He continued, "When you live in the past with its mistakes and regrets, it is hard. I am not there. My name is not I Was. When you live in the future, with its problems and fears, it is hard. I am not there. My name is not I Will Be. When you live in THIS moment, it is not hard. I am here. My name is I Am."

Life can be full and abundant for us when we live in THIS moment. Thinking that way can make all the difference in the world.

It did for me.

Questions for Consideration

1. What do you think about the concept of taking one day at a time?

2. Do you think you live that way in your own life? Do you want to?

3. How could a person develop the mindset of taking one day at a time?

4. What would happen in our lives if we did think that way?

5. Do you believe that if you break your life down to taking one day at a time and if God is with you in each day, nothing can defeat you? If you believed this, how might your life change?

6. What is your "Sabbath" or way of restoring yourself?

Let It All Out

THE VALLEY

My husband, Lord. How difficult it must be to be the "strong one." I worried about him at first, afraid he would keep it all inside, afraid he would not let himself break down and weep. A minister told us that tears are liquid love, and it is so. For weep we must. No, not hysterically or in front of those it would hurt or scare. But there is a soul-level ache that must find release. And so, we weep when we must.

And we call your name.

You know that sometimes I feel angry, Lord. Just plain mad! I'm angry that this is happening to us. I feel "put upon." Sometimes I am so upset at what our family has to face that I feel like I'm suffocating. It isn't fair! You know it's not fair. I'm not *even thinking of the rest of the family now, I'm just thinking that it's not fair to me!*

Lord, help me to get these feelings out so they don't overwhelm me, and help me to put them in the proper perspective.

THE MOUNTAIN

Emotions. What to do with them is such a complex issue, one that people have and will continue to write about *ad infinitum*. One of the important lessons that we learned in dealing with Terry's illness and death was that our emotions were deep and strong, and that they had to find release or they would overwhelm us. This is true for us mortals no matter what life is dealing us. Yes, we gradually learned that we must express our emotions. We've also learned that no two of us expressed our emotions in the exactly same way.

With all the material that has come out about death and dying in the last fifteen or twenty years, we have learned a lot about the grief process. We know there will be stages of denial, anger, grief, etc., but the way each of us goes through the process will be uniquely our own.

The important thing we learned was not to deny what we are feeling and not to discredit what someone else might be feeling. Sometimes our feelings are so strong there is no way we could possibly deny them. There were times after Terry's death when I was sobbing so loudly that I would go into the bathroom and turn on the water in the tub full force so my neighbors wouldn't hear my sobs! We didn't live in an apartment with paper-thin walls, but in a house set back on its own lot.

Sometimes our feelings are not so overt, and these must be faced, too. I, who had never held a gun in my life, kept picturing in my mind's eye taking up a rifle, aiming carefully, and pulling the trigger over and over, blasting away at . . . what? There was never anything to shoot at, but in my anger I wanted to anyway.

There were times when I felt I was emerging from the valley; that life was looking good again, but at the same time my husband was feeling low. I wanted to be impatient with him. Why couldn't he feel as I did? Was he so weak that he couldn't get on with life and appreciate what we DID have?

Of course, a few days later the situation would be reversed, and once again, I was lost in despair. At those times I wondered what was wrong with him. Was he so insensitive that he no longer grieved for our son?

We finally talked about it and we became able simply to allow each other to feel whatever we were feeling. I began to understand how couples who have lost children often end up in divorce courts. My own "caring quotient," that ability to understand another's feelings and respond accordingly, was seriously depleted. It took all my energy just to deal with my own emotions. I simply didn't have enough left to try to understand what any one else was going through.

We wondered if God's hand wasn't on us during this time keeping us from both being at our lowest point at the same time, and therefore being unable to help each other climb out of the despair.

Perhaps the most important thing we learned about our feelings was to let them out. Now, as a person whose emotions are always on the surface anyway (I use my Italian heritage as an excuse) I have long believed in expressing whatever one feels. It was good to have that belief affirmed.

At first I did worry about my husband. As a former Marine officer who was now in railroad management, he had always been an in-charge kind of guy. Thinking back, I remember a practical example a counselor at St. Jude used to teach us a lesson. We were sitting in her office one autumn afternoon talking about how we were dealing with Terry's illness.

She turned to my husband and, taking a large medical book off her desk, she said, "Would you please hold this book in the palm of your hand with your arm outstretched?"

Looking at her quizzically, he replied, "Sure."

He sat there, arm extended, holding the book as we continued to talk.

From time to time the counselor would say, "How are you doing? Would you hold it a little longer please?" Little by little his arm got lower and shakier until finally the book dropped from his hand.

"Now," she said, smiling at him, "wasn't that a relief?"

"Absolutely," he admitted.

"That's the way it is with our feelings," she told us. "If we try to hold them inside they get heavier and heavier. They start to become all we can think about, but when we can get them out we feel a tremendous sense of relief and release." My husband and I have never forgotten that day and that lesson and it's come in handy many times over the years.

Emotions. They play such an important part in what we are. Sometimes people think that expressing emotion is losing control, but I have come to think just the opposite. I have come to believe that when we can express our emotions, when those feelings come spilling out from our depths, we are regaining control of our lives and ourselves. It is when we don't let the feelings out that they grow like a cancer within us and the feelings and emotions control us.

They become so strong within us, whether we admit to them or not, that they are controlling what we are thinking and what we are doing. Everything starts to revolve around them and the effort it takes to keep them under control. It is in the releasing of these emotions that we finally achieve freedom.

There have been recent scientific studies that support this belief. Scientists have found that certain chemicals build up in our bodies during times of stress. When we shed tears these chemicals are released in the tears, and our tension is relieved. We will feel better. As the Scriptures say, "Man is fearfully and wonderfully made" (Psalm 139:14 KJV paraphrased).

Anger is another emotion that can be deadly when denied or turned inward. Studies now show that those who continually suppress anger run a greater risk of heart disease and clinical depression. Sometimes we may suppress our anger because we think it isn't "proper" or appropriate, and we simply deny it. There is a better solution, according to our experts, and that is to identify what is causing the anger and take steps to prevent the situation from happening again. Other than that, they suggest exercise, relaxing hobbies and *talking with a friend* (italics mine.) What better friend do we have than our Lord?

There is another side to this coin of emotions, of course. I believe that it is as important to express joy as it is to express sorrow. I only have to read The Psalms to learn the truth of this. In The Psalms I can see the whole gamut of emotions expressed, from deep lamenting to tremendous joy and peace.

Consider the 6th Psalm:

Lord, don't be angry and rebuke me!
Don't punish me in your anger!

> I am worn out, O Lord; have pity on me. . . .
> I am worn out with grief;
> Every night my bed is damp from my weeping . . .

The psalmist also sings his praises of joy. Psalm 16 says,

> You will show me the path that leads to life:
> Your presence fills me with joy
> And brings me pleasure forever.

Later, in Psalm 27 we read, "With shouts of joy I will offer sacrifices in his Temple. I will sing, I will praise the Lord."

In Psalm 126, ". . . How we laughed, how we sang for joy!"

Both sorrow and joy are part of life, and both should be able to find expression through us in our living with others and in our communicating with our Father. I have always loved the prayer of thanksgiving in Psalm 30:

> Tears may flow in the night
> But joy comes in the morning.

I need the hope of that promise, and I need to be free enough to express joy when I feel it. Aren't we all naturally attracted to people who seem to have a zest for life, who have a smile or a ready laugh for us?

One of my best friends happens to be my mother-in-law, and she has shown me the truth of this. She loves to find fun in a situation, and I think that is what has kept her so young over the years.

My father and stepmother are the same way. Someone, when visiting my home and looking at a picture of my father and stepmother said, "They look like a couple who has a lot of fun in life." And they are. One evening a few years ago I wasn't able to reach them on the phone until quite late. When I finally did get hold of them my dad explained that they'd been at their ballroom dancing class. My father, by the way, was eighty years old at the time. I guess I shouldn't have been surprised when at age ninety he took up cross-country skiing!

This was written a long time ago: "It is a comely fashion to be glad; joy is the grace we say to God." I like that. "Joy is the grace we say to God."

Even the brief glimpse we have of Jesus' life shows me that emotions are to be expressed. We know our Lord felt many emotions and expressed them. Many of those who are required to memorize Bible verses as children confess to choosing John 11:35, "Jesus wept," since it is the shortest Bible verse. This tells us that Jesus expressed His grief at the death of His friend, Lazarus. We know of His anger with the moneychangers in the temple and His gentle joy in little children. We can only sense His anguish at that moment in Gethsemane, but we know He shared it with His Father.

I believe that God wants us to share our emotions, not only with Him, but also with each other. He made us to live in fellowship with each other, but until we are willing to share our real selves with one another we are not living in full fellowship. I think we all need people who are close enough to us so that we are comfortable sharing. Even more, I think He made us to be the ones with whom others can share. We can be the shoulder to cry on, the friend with whom we can celebrate. Releasing our emotions, whether at sorrow or joy, can be what brings us together as children of God.

That can only enrich our lives.

QUESTIONS FOR CONSIDERATION

1. What memories do you have of times you've expressed joy? Sorrow?

2. Are you open to others sharing their emotions with you? Why or why not?

3. Why are many of us uncomfortable when people show emotion? Should we be?

4. What could you do to let others know you are open to them sharing their emotions with you?

5. What are some ways of expressing joy? Sorrow?

CHAPTER 3

Give Thanks...in Everything?

THE VALLEY

I guess we each have our particular turmoil to wrestle. I have found that I can face and deal with the fact that Terry has leukemia. I can face and deal with the fact that he has a rare kind and a poor prognosis. What I cannot deal with is the fact that I could not protect him from this! If a dog attacked him, I would fight with every once of strength to keep the dog from him. If there were a fire, I would whisk him to safety. If there were some hydra-headed monster I would strike and strike until it was killed. And gladly do it, Lord.

But this. THIS! I can't fight it off, and I want to so badly. The anger is there to fight and fight to protect my son . . . but there is nothing to strike at. My hands clench, wanting to strangle this terrible force, but they must remain empty.

Lord, help me to accept all that I must accept.

❖ ❖ ❖

When I used to know mostly joy I thanked you, Lord, for the blessing of sensitivity. I used to say, "I don't mind the valleys. It's worth it in order to know the mountaintops. I used to say that, Lord. I hope I can say it again someday. But for now . . . for now, I wish I could be dulled to this feeling. I don't want to walk this valley, Lord. No mountaintop can take away the deep, dark sadness of this valley. I know I can get through it, but I don't want it! I don't want to travel this way!

Won't you change it, Lord?

※ ※ ※

Remission! REMISSION! What a beautiful word, Lord, and what joy it stirs in us. Our son is in remission; the leukemia is no longer active. I know it's only a temporary thing, but for today, this day, he feels good again. He laughs, Lord, and I will laugh with him.

I know the grim statistics and I know the grim prognosis; but for this day, I rejoice. I have felt your assurance that we will have that hoped for year, that we will have him through his tenth birthday. After that . . . I know, Lord. I know.

But there is today.

TODAY!

※ ※ ※

Lord, I have such strange thoughts sometimes. Today I wished we were past the point of his death, so I could start to deal with it. This waiting for it to happen, wondering when, how, how will we handle it; this is a kind of hell, too. I don't want to wish him away. I want every moment we can have with him. This unknown ahead of me. . . . it scares me so!

Give Thanks... in Everything?

THE MOUNTAIN

Probably the most important and most difficult of all of life's lessons is learning to be thankful in all things, yet we get this very instruction from Scripture. 1 Thessalonians 5:18 tells us to "be thankful in all circumstances." It couldn't be said more clearly, yet that is a scripture with which I have always struggled. How can we possibly be expected to give thanks when terrible things are happening; when our lives seem to be falling apart around us; when tragedy strikes out of the blue?

The fact is that in life we often have to deal with problems and more problems. How do we keep from getting overwhelmed by them? How can we get to that place where we thank God in all things, as Paul wrote to the Thessalonians?

The movie *Awakenings* is an excellent, thought-provoking movie.[1] It deals with the short release from a catatonic state among a group of people who had suffered from encephalitis. In one scene the mother of the first patient to respond to an experimental drug and come "back to life" shares a common reaction. She cries to the doctors that when her son was born and she had a beautiful baby, she never asked "Why? Why did I deserve this wonderful blessing?" Later though, when she could see her son getting worse and worse, she did ask in anguish, "Why? What did I do to deserve this?" I guess I was like that mother.

When they have lost a loved one, I have heard people sometimes say, "Yes. I praise God even for this loss." To me, so encumbered by my humanness, that seemed to be impossible. After Terry's illness and death, I especially questioned whether I could ever feel that way.

Of course, there are many times in our lives when good things happen: marriage, the birth of a child, promotions at work, happy times of sharing, etc. When those things happened to me it was easy for me to say a quick, little prayer of praise to God. Even in small events, I can often remember to thank and praise God. "Thank you, Lord, that I found this missing key." "I praise you, Lord, for this beautiful day."

At those times when what is happening to me is painful and difficult, I struggle with saying "thank you." How can I learn to praise God in *all* things?

In a recent Sunday school lesson on Paul's teachings we were discussing what Paul said about dealing with difficulties. The author of the book we were studying told of a real crisis in his life. He stated that while he did not like the crisis, he liked the opportunity which that crisis gave him.

This philosophy, perhaps, can get me thinking in the right direction. The situation might be terrible and I cannot give thanks for it per se, but when I look at it as an opportunity for growth and for change, I can be thankful for the fact that the opportunity for growth and change can be a positive thing for me.

Perhaps God was trying to teach me that lesson through a minister we once had. Soon after we moved away from his church to another state, his wife died of cancer. We were so sad for him for the terrible loss he and their three young children had suffered. Over the years we've kept in touch at Christmas, and we saw him again a few years ago. In reading his Christmas letters over the years, we felt that he had become a much more compassionate man, ministering in an even greater way than when we were in his congregation. When we got together again he shared that with us himself.

"Going through the experience of losing my wife," he told us, "gave me so much more empathy for people who were suffering. It has made a difference in my ministry."

I don't know if he would say, "Thank you, Lord, that my wife died so young from cancer," but I believe he would say, "Thank you, Lord, for taking that tragic situation and making something good come from it." His life affirms that.

The key, it seems to me, is finding God in whatever situation exists, or at least in knowing that He can bring something good from that situation. He is there, but sometimes it is difficult to find Him. What can I do to recognize His presence?

Already knowing Him can make the difference. When we're in the middle of a bad time, I think it's harder to believe in a loving God. How could He be loving and still allow these terrible things happen to us, we ask ourselves in anguish?

I have a friend whose last few years have contained more heartache than any one person should have to endure in a lifetime. Not only did her husband die at an early age of cancer, but also more recently her son was involved in a terrible, tragic incident for which he is now in prison. She wrote this to me recently, "I must admit that for quite a bit of the last four and a half years I have felt that either we had made God awfully mad, or at the very least, he simply didn't care and had turned his back on our family. I have worked through that now; I guess because I decided there was no acceptable alternative. I don't want to live in a world where there isn't a loving God. I have faith once again and that and Sam's (her son, but not his real name) new-found faith has sustained him and us." She already knew a loving God, so perhaps it was easier for her to find Him again after her despair had separated them. It is logical that if we already have a relationship with a loving Father it will be easier for us to get back to Him when we become lost.

I'm reminded of a lesson on eternal life. My teacher was trying to make the point that while it wasn't up to us to judge who would receive the gift of eternal life, we needed to be concerned about it for ourselves. Sure, some might wait until the last minute to seek salvation, but those of us who have walked with Christ all along will know him well and he will know us well when we get to eternal life. She reminded us how much more comfortable and pleasant it is to be with an old and dear friend than with a stranger. The relationship is closer and much more meaningful.

When we went back to Decatur, Illinois where we had lived fifteen years ago, we gathered with our old Sunday school class, and it was as if we had never left. It brought us so much joy to be with dear friends again. The weekend was one of real pleasure. There was a profound difference between that weekend and other pleasant weekends we have spent with business associates, no matter how lovely the surroundings. The difference was because of the closeness of the relationships.

That lesson nudges me to know Christ now, to be in touch with Him through praying, studying the Bible, being in fellowship with Christians, and trying to learn and grow in my faith. When I am closer to Christ, He is involved more in my day-to-day world. He is not a stranger to me. When I am in a situation that is difficult and my emotions and tears are clouding my vision, knowing the person of Christ will help me to understand, in some way, that I am not alone. I am able to understand that God is there with me in that situation. If that is true, then I can rely on God to bring some good from that situation, no matter how terrible it is. Knowing that, the possibility then exists for me to give thanks in all things; thanks that God is with me and that He can bring some good from that situation.

This, it seems to me, is a slowly learned step-by-step process. First, we must know a personal Christ who makes us confident of God's love for us. Next, we must develop the faith that reassures us that God is with us and that He is involved with us still. If we follow those steps, I believe, we can come to the place of praising God in spite of difficulties.

It is foolish for us to deny the difficulties of life. There are times when life hurts! Leon Uris wrote, "We spend the second half of our life getting over the first half." Perhaps there is truth in that when one considers the popularity of self-help books and articles today. Life can be difficult and we need help in dealing with it. We continue to search for help until we find something in which we can believe, something that is greater than the forces working against us. When we come to know the power of God, we finally understand that we have the help on which we can rely.

I was talking to a friend not long ago. She was telling me the latest news of her family and all of it seemed to be bad. Finally she said, "You know, I wish I could call someone and hear him or her say that everything is just fine. I'm so tired of hearing about problems!" I didn't blame her. The news was pretty discouraging and because she cared about the people, their problems were hurting her too. This is reality.

What I have been learning is I must take that reality, face it, and know that God is in it with me. I have choices I can make, maybe not in my realities and situations, but in the way I will deal with them. It is easier to make choices that involve God if I already know Him and know what He can do. For some people this has been very easy to understand, but it hasn't been so for me. I want to be a deep Christian. I want to have Christ in the center of my life. I want to give thanks in all things, but still I fall short of this. I find some comfort in knowing that perhaps the same was true for Paul when he said, "For even though the desire to do good is in me, I am not able to do it. I don't do the good I want to do; instead, I do the evil that I do not want to do." (Romans 7:18b–19)

Sometimes what separates me from knowing and giving thanks that God is in a situation is that God doesn't do what I want Him to do. It is human nature, I think, that when God's actions aren't what I want or expect, I tend to think He hasn't acted at all. I might bring a situation to God in prayer. In a helpful manner, I usually explain what I want God to do about it. When I see the results I wanted, it's easy for me to give thanks.

However, if my prayer is not acted upon in the way I expect, I have found that I think God has done nothing. Of course if I looked completely honestly at the situation I could see that God had said "No" or perhaps "Later."

There was a wonderful Country and Western song out a few years ago about unanswered prayer. It tells the story of a man who takes his wife to his high school reunion where he meets up with his old high school sweetheart. He recalls how he had prayed for things to work out with his high school flame, but they never did get together. Later he met and married his wife who was really the best choice for him. He thanks God for those unanswered prayers. Of course, they really weren't unanswered. He just thought that because they weren't answered the way he wanted at the time.[2]

It was some time before I learned that lesson in regard to Terry's death. I had prayed so hard for Terry, and so many of all kinds of religious persuasions prayed so hard, that I really thought God would work a miracle and let Terry live. For a while his death spoke to me of unanswered prayer. I couldn't understand why God hadn't answered our prayers, but I only knew that He hadn't. I thought that there must be some failing in my faith; that it just wasn't strong enough.

Finally, the realization came to me that God HAD answered our prayers, but He had not answered them in the way I wanted. I had prayed for Terry to be well again, and he is. God did lift Terry from that bed of suffering and brought him to a wholeness that I cannot even begin to understand in this life. We had prayed that we would get through the ordeal, and we have. God has helped us grow in our spiritual lives and in our sensitivity to others through the experience of Terry's illness and death. Although 70–90% of couples that lose a child to death end up with the extra burdens of divorce or alcohol and/or drug abuse, we have been able to avoid those problems. Now, looking back, I can clearly see that God's kept His hand on our shoulders every step of the way through other people and through the indwelling of the Holy Spirit.

This is the strength and comfort I know exists. I can claim this for whatever lies ahead. It is that strength and comfort for which I can give thanks. This is what I want to share with others. Giving thanks in everything is a way of reminding me, or making me aware, of God's presence in my life. It reminds me of my deep dependence on God. As I am able to focus more on God, I find myself focusing less on the circumstances that might defeat me.

I find tremendous comfort in recognizing the constancy of God. When life is full of rough seas we need the security of a pier on which to lash those vulnerable little boats of our lives. God is that pier, steady and secure. When I know there is the constancy of God, no matter what the circumstances, it is easier for me to give thanks in all situations. I can give thanks for that constancy that was with me yesterday, is with me today, and will be with me tomorrow.

I have a framed calligraphy of Romans 8:28 up in my house as a reminder, and I do seem to need a lot of reminders. The words are clear: "And we know that in all things God works for the good of those who love Him." The key phrase is "in *all* things." If we can really believe that, then we do have the foundation for giving thanks in *all* things.

The prayer of Reinhold Niebuhr that has become known as the Serenity Prayer holds special meaning for me. "Oh, God, give me the serenity to accept what cannot be changed, courage to change what should be changed, and wisdom to distinguish the one from the other."[3]

When difficulties come to us, I think it is our nature to fight against them, to try and change those difficulties, to be in control of what is happening to us. Sometimes we can do that. Sometimes we can't. I think it is important to know the difference. I have wasted so much emotional energy trying to change situations over which I have no control. If I had been able to focus on God in those situations, if I could have given thanks for His presence and His ability to bring some good from those circumstances, I could have gone on with my life in a better fashion.

I am finally coming to realize that to give thanks in all things is possible if I focus on the God of strength who is with me in all times, rather than focusing on the situation and what I can do about it. Psalm 46 reminds us, "God is our shelter and strength, always ready to help in times of trouble" (Psalm 46:1). This message is present throughout the Scriptures for me. It is evidenced in the lives of Christians.

Give Thanks... in Everything?

Recently, my sister made a video of all the old 16mm home movies our dad had taken of us when we were growing up. The color has faded over the years and the pictures aren't as clear as they used to be, but we don't care. It was *our* childhood and watching the video brought back so many memories.

My absolute favorite is one little scene shot during the time we lived in New Mexico as young children. My older sister and I are climbing up a very steep rocky hillside, so steep that we are almost crawling. When I reach the top I turn to the beautiful vista in front of me, and exuberantly I lift my arms toward heaven. It is a common gesture of joyful children, but to me it is such an affirmation of finding and celebrating the joy that is there for us. Life can be hilly and rocky, difficult to climb, but we can get to that point where we can see the beauty of the abundant life God gives us. The only appropriate response is the exultation of praise and thanksgiving.

I now know that God is indeed with me no matter what is happening to me and I can finally understand what it means to give thanks in all things. Yes, I still miss Terry and some part of me wishes God had done things my way. I often wish He would have made Terry well and let me keep him here. Even so I can thank God for being with us in that situation, for blessing our lives with Terry for ten years, for healing him of his suffering, and, ultimately, for changing and helping us grow spiritually.

Give thanks . . . in everything? Yes, I guess it really has become possible for me.

QUESTIONS FOR CONSIDERATION

1. Do you think we are really supposed to "give thanks in all things?"

2. Are you able to give God thanks in everything? If not, in what areas are you not able to give thanks?

3. What might you do to be more willing to give God thanks?

4. How would your life change if you were able to thank God in all things?

5. Have there been examples of any people in your life who have the mindset of giving thanks to God in all things?

CHAPTER 4

Reach Out and Touch Someone

THE VALLEY

I have a whole new understanding of "it is more blessed to give than to receive." I don't like being the receiver, Lord! People have been so thoughtful and generous. Of course, I appreciate the gifts. It's just that I hate being the one in need. I want to say, ". . . but there's been some mistake. I don't need. . . ." But there hasn't been a mistake and I DO need, and that is so painful!

❖ ❖ ❖

Today some of the Detroit Lions came by the hospital to take a few publicity pictures so they can raise money for the work of St. Jude. Our son was chosen to be in the pictures. Everyone is smiling and acting as though it were such a pleasant activity, but I'm not smiling inside, Lord. That's my son in

the pictures. MY SON, my blond-headed first-born son! He is the one who has leukemia!
It breaks my heart, Lord. It just makes me want to weep.

❖ ❖ ❖

The Mountain

One of the lessons we learned during the time of Terry's illness and death was how important it was to have other people show they cared. I learned several things about reaching out to others during that time. First of all I learned how very important the act of reaching out to others really is.

In the very beginning of our ordeal, before we knew that Terry had leukemia, he had only seemed sick with flu-like symptoms. I had taken him to the pediatrician who ran some blood tests and sent us home. Once home, I received a call from his office to come in with my husband but to leave Terry at home. Terrified, I called Merle Ridout, our minister's wife who was a close friend and neighbor, and asked if she could stay with Terry and Kile while I went to the doctor's. She came right over.

At the office, our pediatrician explained that Terry had a serious blood disease, perhaps leukemia, and we should take him immediately to one of three special hospitals he named.

"If it were your child, which hospital would you choose?" asked my husband.

"St. Jude Children's Research Hospital," was his immediate reply.

He left us alone for a few minutes to try and absorb this terrifying blow. Our concern was not to upset our boys too much, so I called our minister's wife to explain the news to her, rather than do it when we got home where Terry would hear and sense our panic. With fear in our hearts, we drove home.

At the door of our house stood Ed Ridout, our minister, waiting to hug us and help us make plans. I will never forget the comfort of having someone there, some tangible strength to touch as we felt we were falling wildly through space.

Our lives have never been the same. The memory of that day is filled with absolute anguish, terror, and frustration, yet there is also the memory of others caring, others there for us, others reaching out because of Christian love and concern. Now I see that God was there that day also. If it had not been so, I think the whole course of our dealing with everything would have been completely different.

People reached out to us in a myriad of ways during the fifteen months of Terry's illness. The diversity of their expressions speaks to me of the wonderful way in which God has made each person unique and different.

Sometimes we would need to be at St. Jude in Memphis for extended periods of time. We would return to our home in Roanoke, Virginia to find our yard mowed and never learn who had done it. Some expressed their caring by bringing a meal during an exhausting time for us, or finding interesting things for Terry to read or play with during the lonely times he had to spend in bed. Our minister and his wife, Ed and Merle Ridout, often provided a second home for Kile during that time so his life could continue with some sense of routine. When Terry was in remission we tried to keep his life as normal as possible. His scout leaders, teachers, Sunday school teachers, friends, and neighbors all helped make that possible.

On one occasion, a lady from our church stopped by with a beautiful bouquet of roses from her garden. We sat and visited a short while, and then she went on her way. Every time I looked at that bright arrangement on the kitchen table I felt as though someone had hugged me and said, "I care. You are not alone."

God gives each of us talents and abilities and we can use these in a powerful way to reach out to others. Whether we are on the receiving end or the giving end, this is something we need desperately.

In the few years after Terry's death I had a few people say to me, "We felt so badly about your situation. We wanted to do something, but we just didn't know what to do or say." I understand that feeling because I've had it myself when others have had a loss, yet, I'm also aware that at the time they made me feel that they didn't care enough to be there when I needed them. Even though I understood with my mind why they weren't there, I felt with my heart that they had let me down. It seems when we're going through a crisis, we're more apt to react with our hearts or feelings rather than with our minds or intellect.

Paul's letters remind us so often of our responsibility one to another. He says, "The only obligation you have is to love one another. Whoever does this has obeyed the Law" (Romans 13:8). When we feel that love toward one another we are able to find ways to say, "I care," whether it be with words or actions.

One Sunday after Terry first went into remission, I was making my way to a pew at church when a young mother I knew slightly came up and hugged me. She didn't say a word, but her action spoke volumes to me of shared joy in that small, temporary victory of Terry's remission.

Sometimes, the only thing we can do for someone is pray. I have learned not to discount that because it can make a real difference. I used my learning experience about prayer as the basis for an article I wrote that first appeared in *Decision* magazine.[1] I have received letters from the far corners of the world in response to that article from people who knew the power of intercessory prayer themselves.

My experience happened in 1967. My Marine husband, Frank Kile, was serving thirteen months in Viet Nam. I had stayed in California, far away from family, because it seemed best for us for several reasons. We kept busy, and the days moved along slowly. Sundays, though, were the worst. Sunday had always been a family day. When Frank Kile had been home, after church we would enjoy special afternoon family activities like a picnic or a trip to the park or the beach. With my husband gone, Sundays dragged by. All our friends were busy with their own families.

I think I missed Frank Kile most during the worship service. When he had been with me I would slip my hand into his, or he would gently rest his arm around my shoulders. I felt secure and content in those moments. Worshipping in God's house with my husband by my side was a rich and tangible blessing. With him gone, not knowing exactly where he was or what was happening to him made the emptiness even more forceful.

One Sunday morning was different. I had gone through the usual frantic routine of trying to get the baby and three-year-old Terry ready for church on time. As I finally settled into the pew, my thoughts turned to my husband and how much I missed him. During the anthem I felt especially alone and despondent. Suddenly, it was as if an arm, Someone's arm, was placed gently around my shoulders again! I nestled into the comfort. A sense of peace, of real contentment, filled me. That warm, secure feeling stayed with me throughout the service.

Afterward, as I was getting ready to leave, a church friend came up to me and said, "I want you to know I prayed for you today."

"Why, thank you!" I replied, somewhat surprised. I had never thought about someone praying for me.

"I looked at you sitting there alone during the anthem, and I know how much you must miss your husband and how you must worry about his being in Viet Nam. So, I prayed that Jesus would surround you with his love and give you peace."

I looked at her in astonishment. "During the anthem? I felt it! I really did!" For the first time in my life I understood something about intercessory prayer. It was more than a hopeful phrase. It was real, as real as the comfort of an arm around my shoulder. Knowing that has made a difference for me in my life.

Intercessory prayer is a good way to begin when we reach out to others. In some circumstances that might be our only way to respond, but I believe that it should only be the beginning. We have a responsibility to use the gifts God gave us to find other ways to reach out.

We have the perfect example of Christ before us. He reached out to people where they were hurting, whether it be from their own illness, the death of a loved one, loneliness, heartache, emptiness, whatever.

God did not just give us Christ's example and then expect us to follow it using our own inner strength and will. Paul explains how God gave us the Holy Spirit to guide us as individuals. "There are different kinds of spiritual gifts, but the same Spirit gives them. There are different ways of serving, but the same Lord is served. There are different abilities to perform service, but the same God gives ability to everyone for their particular service. The Spirit's presence is shown in some way in each person for the good of all" (I Corinthians 12:4–7). I have learned how important it is to take the ability God has given each of us and use it to say to our hurting brothers and sisters, "God cares and I care, too."

I have come to understand that when I see someone else in pain, I must respond. Sometimes there are small practical things I can do: help with a meal, run an errand, provide transportation. Sometimes there is nothing practical I can do, so I need to call on the phone, send a card, stop by for a visit to say "hello." These are things I need to do, not just for the sake of others, but also for myself. Deep inside each of us is a need to reach out and make contact with others. A wonderful Bible leader of mine once said, "Every Christian has a gift for someone else."

However, I have found that there are times when it is not easy for me to reach out. Perhaps I don't know the person well and I don't feel comfortable. Perhaps their problem is something that is private and they don't want public expressions of concern. Perhaps the crisis is happening to someone I don't like very much or someone I don't know at all. I am a shy person by nature, and in these situations I simply would like to avoid reaching out at all. Do I have to? Is it really necessary for me to respond to every situation of which I am made aware?

Several years ago I had the opportunity to hear a dedicated and active nun lead a workshop. She had spent a great deal of time in Nicaragua and El Salvador and she shared her experiences in trying to make social justice a reality. I'll never forget the powerful way she spoke.

She said, "We don't talk enough about how we understand God, because how we understand God affects what we do. We need to understand God in an *inclusive* way." (Italics mine.)

She touched my heart that day. Her message to me was that I must look at all people in an inclusive way, and in so doing, I will come to care about them. With my caring comes a response, a response that will be unique to me because of the gifts and graces God has given to me. No one can respond to all the needs, but because the Holy Spirit is guiding me, I will respond to those needs of others to which I am able to respond.

What I have learned in my own life since that day is that when I am closer in line with God's love and will for my life, I am better able to see the needs of others to which I can respond. I am better able to find a way to respond.

I was fortunate to meet a very special woman in Birmingham, Alabama, a minister who had been the catalyst in starting an excellent program to meet the needs of the homeless. As she told how it all came about, she said, "I believe in the 'at least theology.'" She says to herself, "I can't solve world hunger and I can't cure homelessness, but *at least* I can gather some volunteers together to serve a meal to the homeless." With that beginning, she created the possibility for the excellent program that has evolved. God gives each of us talents and abilities so that *at least* we can do something.

I am someone who loves the Christmas season. I love all the special church activities focusing on this special event in our Christian year. I love all the secular activities as well. The idea of gifting is a favorite of mine. I spend all year trying to think of the perfect gift for each loved one and I love opening the surprises they have chosen for me.

I find much joy in the generous caring we all seem to have at Christmas, giving to those less fortunate, those who have so many needs. I heard someone say once, "Christmas shows us what can happen to a world when Christ enters into it." That means something to me. It says that when Christ enters the world there is love, there is caring, there is reaching out to others. Perhaps this is what the nun was saying to me that day. Christ's love can enter the world through us. Our world seems like a better place every year at Christmas. It can be like that any day—every day—when I let that love come through me and reach out to someone who needs it. Because Christ first loved me, I have the love to give to someone else.

One of the colleges which received a past year's Call To Prayer and Self Denial offering of United Methodist Women has this motto: "We receive to give." That makes good sense in our laws of natural physics. Picture a test tube in a chemistry lab. As you pour water into the opening at the top, the tube fills up. If just left like that, it would stagnate, but now picture the tube with an additional spout on the side. As the water is poured in, the tube fills and the same water flows out of the spout.

I think that this is the way that God intends for me to be. He fills me with His love, but it is only when that love is poured out through me that I am kept vital and alive. I not only need to receive from others, but I need to give myself. It has been said, "Don't become so heavenly-minded that you're no earthly good." That might happen if I were only concerned with getting the flowing love of God's Word and keeping it within the test tube of myself. To be any "earthly good" that love must flow on through me to others.

There was something else I learned from the experience of people reaching out to us during Terry's struggle with leukemia. I learned how very painful it is to be the recipient.

I've always liked the idea of reaching out to others. I found it extremely difficult to be on the other side. To be in need can be demoralizing and so destructive to one's sense of dignity and worth. This is not to say that I didn't appreciate the gifts. They meant so much to us, and yet it hurt so much to be the one in need.

Although St. Jude never sent a bill, the cost of travel and other special needs devastated our finances. My husband was able to continue with his good job, but even so there were two occasions when we got down to our last dollars. The first time, my husband and I sat together going over our finances and admitted that we would probably have to ask for help for our next trip to St. Jude. The next morning's mail brought a generous check from my aunt.

The next time, without even going over our finances, we knew that we had nothing left. That evening our minister came by to sit and talk for awhile. Before leaving he said, "By the way, the congregation took a special offering and wants you to have this," as he handed us an envelope with another extremely generous check. We were overwhelmed, touched so deeply by their thoughtfulness and generosity. At the same time, we hated the fact that we needed it.

"I know you'll repay it by helping someone else who needs it later on when you're able to," he added. This was what we needed to hear, and it's something we've tried to do. What Ed taught us that evening was that when we give gifts and reach out to others we need to do it in a way that is loving, and that considers their dignity. I learned through our experience that I needed to be very careful in how I reach out so that it feels like a hug and not a slap.

I was reminded, with a sense of shame, of an early experience I had in trying to help another. I was a new wife on the military base and because of my background in social work, a lady from our church asked me to accompany her visiting a family our church had been helping. She had been working with a young mother of several children whose youngest child had cystic fibrosis. They were struggling to make ends meet on her husband's low corporal's pay. I was uncomfortable about going because I didn't know anything about cystic fibrosis, but I read up on what little I could find about it at the library, and I agreed to go. Hoping to appear more mature and experienced than I was, (I was twenty-three years old) I dressed up in my Sunday clothes and high heels. It must have appeared that I pranced in and instead of listening, I told the young woman several ways she could cut back on expenses and do better. Afterwards, she told the lady from our church *never* to bring me there again, and I didn't blame her. I had tried to cover my lack of knowledge of her situation with confident-sounding suggestions. I wanted to be helpful and I didn't think I had anything to offer but practical suggestions. I was so wrong! If I had approached her with love and concern for her situation I would have seen so many ways I could have been helpful to her. I cringe as I remember that situation, but I'm thankful that I learned from it.

For as long as my mother lived, she had a lovely framed needlework on the wall of her home. Her best friend had done it in their early years, and it had these words stitched in tiny careful stitches, "Friendship Is a Sheltering Tree." It pictured a tree whose branches reached out, umbrella-like, to cover the whole picture. I've always loved that saying because it has such a peace-giving, secure sound to it. I think that God is telling me that is the kind of friendship I need to feel toward people. He wants me to have a friendship in which I can reach out and as I do, I shield the other person from the rains of life that fall on all of us.

My mother also taught me an important lesson during that difficult time in our lives. I was sharing with her some of the kindness that was offered to us, but I was also letting her know that I didn't like being on the receiving end.

She said, "Now listen, you need to accept those things others offer, because they need to give them. This isn't just happening to you, you know. Dealing with Terry's leukemia is happening to all of us, your family and your friends. Let others feel like there is something they can do, because they need that." At the time, I really didn't appreciate my mother's advice, but I knew, deep down, that she was right.

I have a friend who does things for others all the time, but she absolutely does not let anyone do things for her. I find this so frustrating. I guess that is the other side of the coin.

I am a lifetime member of Weight Watchers® (struggle, struggle). In one of their ads a few years ago they used a wonderful story.

> One very hot day, a little boy was trying to move a huge stone. His face was flushed and streaked with sweat as he pushed the stone that would not budge. His father came along and paused, "Son, are you doing the best you can?"
>
> The boy straightened up in surprise. "Of course I am, Father," he said indignantly.
>
> His father persisted: "But are you sure you're doing your best?"
>
> Without a word, the little boy got a new hold on the rock, bent his knees, and made another mighty effort, but the stone was too big. "See, Dad?" he said, showing he had done his best without success.

"But you still aren't doing the best you can," his father insisted, "Because you haven't asked me to help you."[2]

There are times when we need to ask for help. It happens to each of us at sometime in our lives. I had a hard time struggling with this during Terry's illness. I could have saved myself some turmoil if I had simply recognized it and let God help, reaching out to me through those around me.

Reaching out and touching someone is not only a good telephone company motto, but it is also an important Christian principle. Not only do we have Christ's example, but we also have the example of countless Christians over generations and the mandate in our Scriptures.

The prayer attributed to St. Francis of Assisi because it shows his spirit of love and service to Christ (although it actually is of unknown origin probably from around 1915) expresses so well what we should be doing when we reach out.

> Lord,
> Make me an instrument of Thy peace;
> Where there is hatred, let me sow love;
> Where there is injury, pardon;
> Where there is doubt, faith;
> Where there is despair, hope;
> Where there is darkness, light;
> And where there is sadness, joy.
> O Divine Master,
> Grant that I may not so much seek to be consoled, as to console;
> To be understood, as to understand;
> To be loved, as to love;
> For it is in giving that we receive,
> It is in pardoning that we are pardoned,
> And it is in dying that we are born to eternal life.[3]

Questions for Consideration

1. Have you ever been on the receiving end of "reaching out? How did it make you feel?

2. In what ways have you reached out to others?

3. What are some of the gifts God has given you that you can use to reach out others?

4. How can we know the needs of others?

5. What action might you take if you were to initiate the "at least" theology?

CHAPTER 5

The Best Day of My Life

THE VALLEY

It is summertime again, Lord. Today Terry was in his first golf tournament, and they awarded him the Sportsmanship Trophy. He told me it was the greatest moment of his life. Thank you, Lord, that he could have that moment. To work hard at something and to gain recognition for that work—that is fulfillment. What more could we wish for our children, Lord?

❖ ❖ ❖

We have such good times as a family. Tonight we all went ice-skating together. It's been a complete year since Terry first became ill. It's been the worst year of our lives, but it's been a good year, too. We have so much love and joy that we share. We tease each other. We laugh together. Sometimes, we weep together, too, Lord. But we love—we love, and so we feel all *the good and bad together. I wouldn't want it any other way, Lord.*

❖ ❖ ❖

Our son has never quit. He has been hiking in wilderness areas, and now he's back in school—a fifth grader! He is active in Scouts and he's started as an acolyte at church. When I watch him go forward to light the candles at church, I am filled with pride in him because of his courage and strength.

Next week is his tenth birthday. I knew we'd have this past year with him. I am grateful and at peace.

❖ ❖ ❖

THE MOUNTAIN

There was one time when Terry was at St. Jude that he became ill with encephalitis. Other diseases, especially pneumonia, plague leukemia-stricken children, and this one had settled in with a vengeance. We had to keep the shades down because even the normal light was so painful. His feet were so tender that he couldn't bear the weight of a sheet on them. It was a grim time.

We could only sit beside him, anguishing, praying, and willing him toward health. Each day the doctors would just shake their heads. "We're doing all we can," they'd say.

Finally, one day, I felt that Terry could stand a little light, and I searched for minute indications of improvement. "We'll just have to wait and see," said the doctors.

Terry began to inch his way back, but once he'd started I knew he could make it, and he did. As time went on he could sit up in bed, then, later, be moved to a wheelchair.

When we took him home, the doctors said, "He may never be able to walk again."

We tried to fill his days with home schooling, working with his stamp collection, observing his fish, watching TV, anything, but Terry wanted more. "Mom and Dad, I know I can walk again," he said.

I remember standing outside his room, listening, gripping my hands together to keep from rushing in, as I could hear him dropping out of bed, then pulling himself up in his wheelchair. Each time, he would move the wheel chair further and further from the bed, crawling the difference in between. As he got stronger, he began to take fledgling steps. Eventually, he did it! He not only walked again, but he rode his bike, and even went on some hikes in the nearby Blue Ridge Mountains. What a lesson he taught us about courage and determination! He reminded me about believing in possibilities.

Now, so many more years into maturity than I was then, I am really beginning to believe that therein lies a secret for life. When we believe in possibilities we're not afraid to forge ahead, to try new roads, to stretch our minds. That, I think, is what our loving Father wants for us, that we can become more than we are.

Believing in possibilities is, to me, the message of the New Testament. Without Christ, as we struggle on our own, we will always fall short. Paul's message to us through his letters is that our own efforts are not enough to earn us that which we need most for completeness, salvation, or oneness with God. Yet God's grace, His gift to us, gives us possibilities beyond our deepest yearnings.

The story of the rich young ruler is an example from the Scriptures. The rich young ruler comes to Jesus asking how to receive eternal life. When Jesus answers, the young ruler says, "But I already do those things." Jesus then gives him instructions with which the young ruler cannot bring himself to comply. The disciples are concerned, wondering at their own chances to be saved.

"Who can then be saved?" they ask. Jesus looks straight at them and answers, "This is impossible for man, but for God everything is possible" (Matthew 19:25b, 26).

And further in Mark, there is the story of Jesus healing the boy with an evil spirit. The father begs Jesus to help them, and Jesus responds that he can help them, ". . . if you yourself can! Everything is possible for the person who has faith" (Mark 9:23).

What a wonderful message! Everything is possible for the person who has faith! If this is true, there is no end to what we might accomplish or what an amazing life we could lead. This is a powerful message to me, yet it is one I have found myself not daring to believe over the years. This message tells me that as I align myself closer to God's will for my life, endless possibilities open up to me. Yes, there are things I can do and achieve by pure grit and determination on my part, but these possibilities are multiplied a thousand times over when I put my hand in God's and go forward in that partnership.

I think of Moses as he was called to lead the Israelites out of Egypt. His first response was, "Who, me?"

God didn't say, "Hey, Moses, it'll be a piece of cake. No problem." Instead He said something even better. He said, "I will be with you." What a wonderful, awesome promise. "I will be with you." That is as much a promise to me and to you as it was to Moses. With God, Moses' possibilities became so much more. With God, so do mine.

Terry taught me a lot about believing in possibilities, and dealing with his terminal illness taught me a lot about what we want for our children. The golf tournament he was in really made that message clear to me.

I'll never forget that golf tournament. Terry continued with golf when he got sick so that he could have some sports outlet that was a non-contact sport. He had a small set of golf clubs that had been cut down to his size, and he and his dad would play at the local nine-hole golf course whenever possible. He wasn't a strong hitter, but would manage to get the ball straight down the fairway. His younger brother, Kile, was often his caddie.

During the time he was recovering from encephalitis and was still wheelchair bound, he continued to try to play golf. His dad would lift him from the wheelchair to the golf cart, and each time he needed to hit the ball, his dad would lift him from the golf cart and hold him until he could stand steadily enough to swing at the ball.

Golf became very important to him. He read about the Junior Golf Tournament in our hometown of Roanoke, Virginia, and he was determined to play in it.

"But, Terry, you've never even played eighteen holes, much less thirty-six," I protested weakly.

"I can do it," he insisted. His dad called and made arrangements for him to be able to ride a golf cart in the tournament.

The first day of the tourney dawned bright and beautiful. Kile and I watched Terry play the first hole. It was disaster! He was very nervous, and I was even worse. His first shot went into the rough and things didn't get much better after that. He completed that first hole with a score of thirteen. I felt like weeping. Silently I wondered why he was putting himself through this. I wanted to explain to everyone watching what a tremendous victory it was for him even to be there playing. I couldn't bear to think that anyone might be looking at him and judging him in a negative way.

I met him when he took a quick break before playing the back nine. His face was streaked with sweat and he looked so tired. "How's it going?" I asked.

He just smiled. "OK" was all he said. He drank a Coke quickly and went on. The official who was driving the golf cart said, "He's hanging in there."

Of course, I didn't have any idea what that meant. Was he just enduring it? Was he doing better? Worse? In my heart I wanted him to do really well. I wanted him to win. I wanted him to have some acclamation, where the world would look at him and applaud. He deserved it.

The tournament went its appointed thirty-six holes in two days. Terry managed to complete the whole course. And his final score? I don't even know; it didn't matter. At the awards ceremony there was a large special Sportsmanship Trophy with Terry's name on it. Amidst the applause, he walked up proudly to receive it and I rejoiced with him.

That night, with the trophy shining on his bedside table, he told me, "This was the best day of my life."

My heart overflowed with grateful prayer that night. I had learned that day that sometimes the things we want for our children, and for ourselves, are not the things we most need or deserve. I had wanted Terry to win that tournament, to have the best score. If he couldn't have that, I had wanted to whisk him away to a safer place, where nothing was risked and therefore nothing was lost.

But for Terry, to play his best was to win, and that's what he did. The trying was what was important. Terry wasn't in competition with the other young people; he was in competition within himself, to have his strongest side win, to live the possibility. What more could we want for our children? What more could we want for ourselves?

I think that God was trying to teach me that lesson through Terry. It's still hard for me to learn. We have two sons now, Kile and Joel. I want so much for them in their lives; I want all the good things that could possibly come to them. I still catch myself praying for good things for them, and then I am reminded that what I should be praying for is simply that they live in God's will for their lives. Then the possibilities that are best for them will be there.

Our youngest son is about to graduate from college as I write this. I have no idea what he will do after graduation. I do know that he walks with a living Lord, and so I know that wonderful possibilities exist for him. I don't pray that he will do a specific thing or go to a specific place, but I pray that he continues his partnership with God so that his possibilities are the best.

What do I wish for our sons? Yes, I wish for all good things, but even more I wish and pray that their strongest side wins. I wish that side of them that is the best, that can reach the farthest, that believes the most, that comes the closest to Christ. I pray that side of them is victorious. Sometimes that can't happen without struggle, without taking a risk.

I have placed each of our boys tenderly in God's hands and by doing that, I believe, they can both experience, like Terry, the best days of their lives.

Yes, there are times I try to snatch them back, to take control, to manipulate this way or that. There are times when I fall short and simply leave God out of things all together, but I'm trying. When I remember Terry's face as he looked at his trophy one last time before I turned out the light, I want to try. I really do.

Questions for Consideration

1. What has been the best day of your life? Why was it the best?

2. In your heart of hearts, what is it you want for your children?

3. What message did you get from your parents about what they wanted for you in your life?

4. How do you determine what you want most in life?

5. What might others say was most important to you?

CHAPTER 6

There's No Such Thing as Pixie Dust

THE VALLEY

We thought you had sprinkled pixie dust on us, Lord. Our lives since we have been married have been good and richly abundant. We have known you and served you through the church. Everything we tried turned out well. We had so many blessings. Were we smug about them, Lord? I guess so. I guess so.

It seems that we thought following you made us immune to the heartaches of life. But it doesn't work that way, does it?

I remember the story of the caterpillar, struggling through the debris on the ground. But as a butterfly, he flies right over the debris and problems. We're like that, aren't we, Lord? We struggle and struggle to get through the debris of life. Yet when we truly know you and trust you, we become like the butterfly. The problems are still there, but we can deal with them through a completely new perspective.

Lord, please help me to be a butterfly.

He has gone for a routine check up. For once, I am not afraid. I joke with a friend. The phone rings—my husband—relapse again, he says. It can't be! Now there is no hope.

I can't believe it, Lord. I thought a year was a long time, but it wasn't. It was only . . . only the blink of an eye, only the flash of sunlight on a rippling brook.

But we still have today. I will live every today with him until the days are all gone.

Help me, Lord. Please help me!

THE MOUNTAIN

I don't know where I got the idea that living life as a Christian would make me safe from the blows of the world, but somewhere along the way in my earlier years I think the smugness of that idea had seeped into my unconsciousness. It wasn't that I was really getting that information from somewhere as much as the cause-and-effect situations that were happening in my life made me believe that way.

God had really blessed us. Since my husband and I had married, life had been really good. Our first home was in southern California where my husband, Frank Kile, was a Marine officer. We both agreed that the church was an important part of our lives and we found a Methodist Church in each of our transfers in which we could find meaningful involvement. We served as youth counselors at several of the churches and those relationships we had with young people added so much to our lives.

Frank Kile enjoyed his work and activities with the Marine Corps, and I loved being a stay-at-home wife and then mother as first Terry was born, followed by a miscarriage, then by Kile three years later.

When I think about the first ten years of our married life, the moments and events flip through my mind like pages of a photo album. I see the glistening of the sun caught in the drops of the sprinkler as Terry toddles after our dog, Misty, in the backyard. There is laughter in the air. I never think of our California days without thinking of sunshine, not just the kind that warms the skin, but the kind that warms the heart as well. I remember how it felt to sit by my husband during the church service and slip my hand into his.

I remember Disneyland, and ball games, cookouts, and Olvera Street, and, of course, the beach. I can picture those special young people from our church sitting all around the floor of our tiny living room, asking questions, sharing faith.

Frank Kile had to leave for his thirteen months in Viet Nam just six weeks before Kile was born. It wasn't an easy time, but we felt strong, in fact, we felt invincible. I stayed in our home in California rather than go east to be near family. We thought that Terry's life would be upset enough with his dad gone for a year and a new baby in the home, so by staying in California at least we could keep him from being completely uprooted. Besides, I loved it there. I felt safe and secure.

When it was time for Frank Kile's R & R in Hawaii, I was able to go and take both boys. Our minister had been transferred to Hawaii, so while we were there he was to baptize Kile. It just so happened that the *Los Angeles Times* was doing a series on families meeting for R & R at that time, and because of the baptism they asked to include us in the article. They managed to get a picture of Frank Kile's first look at Kile, who was then five months old. What a wonderful moment to have on film! We never asked ourselves, "Why us, Lord?" We just expected good things to happen to us.

In spite of being in Vietnam during 1967 and '68 and at DaNang during the Tet Offensive, Frank Kile returned home safely from his tour of duty in Viet Nam. I can still picture that day. I wore a new red suit I had made and the boys were dressed in their Sunday best. The house was spotless with fresh bunches of yellow mums in bowls on the tables. While we were waiting for the plane to land at El Toro Marine Air Station near our home, I couldn't help but notice a couple who seemed extremely anxious. I overheard them explain that their son had called to say that he would be on the next flight, and they had met each flight for three days with no sign of him nor any word from him. As the plane first came into view we were all pressed against the glass for that first view, that first look that would tell us everything was all right.

The plane settled on the runway and taxied slowly toward us. Finally the door was opened, and the men hurried out. Frank Kile was the very first one off, and we rushed across the distance that separated us. Somehow, he held all three of us at once. He was really there, home again!

Later, after the necessary paperwork was completed, we walked to our car. I looked back and saw the couple I had noticed before was leaving also, without their son, the mother weeping, the father with his arm around her. We went home in joy and I never once said, "Why us, Lord? What did we do to deserve this?"

Frank Kile's next duty station was Norfolk, Virginia, so we packed up and headed east. In those days a move meant a sense of adventure, a new place. While living in Norfolk, Frank Kile got out of the Marine Corps and into the operating management end of the railroad industry. It meant starting over with two children, but we weren't afraid. We expected everything to work out well for us, and it did.

Frank Kile worked hard, advanced, and got transferred a lot. We went on to Moberly, Missouri, where we loved our little home in the country; Peru, Indiana followed and finally, Roanoke, Virginia.

I especially loved Roanoke. My heart had always been in Virginia. It was where I had gone to college, where I had my first job as a juvenile probation officer, and where we were married. The area around Roanoke has a beauty that is unequaled anywhere. The rolling foothills of the Blue Ridge Mountains, the farmlands, the streams and forests of hardwoods all somehow speak to my soul and lift my spirit. Life was good there.

The boys were growing, happy, healthy, and fun. We loved our home on top of a hill with good neighbors for socializing and beautiful mountain views when we wanted solitude. Yes, life was very good there. Still, we never asked, "Why, Lord? What did we do to deserve this?"

That's when it happened, the day that changed our lives forever, the words that made it all seem to come tumbling down. "Your son has leukemia." Then we asked, "Why? Why us?" Then we wanted to understand about God and His justice. Then we wanted answers.

Paul has taught me so much about understanding how God's love filters through the trials of life to touch us in a way that helps and heals, that restores and redeems.

Paul, himself, was not immune to difficulties. We read about the "thorn in his flesh" in his letters. "Three times I have prayed to the Lord about this and asked Him to take it away" (2 Corinthians 12:8), he writes. Somehow, I've always felt that if Paul, with his tremendous impact on Christianity, still had difficulties to endure, how could I expect not to have them? Paul didn't end by just mentioning his problems. He told us his Lord's response: "But His answer was: 'My grace is all you need, for my power is strongest when you are weak.'" Then Paul went on to explain that he was content with his weakness if that meant that Christ would be strong in him. Paul's circumstances didn't change, but his attitude did.

Paul's words strongly bring home to me the point that my Sunday school teacher made to me about the butterfly so many years before. She shared with our class about the difficult time of her long illness. It had devastated the family financially and that had put great strains upon the relationship with her husband and children. One day she dragged herself out to sit on her back steps. Sitting there, feeling miserable about her situation, her eye caught a slight movement on the ground. A caterpillar was struggling and struggling to get through some debris of twigs and leaves. "Foolish caterpillar," she thought. "If it would only wait until it's a butterfly, it could fly over all that debris." Suddenly, the insight God was revealing jumped out at her! She was like that caterpillar, struggling and struggling against the debris in her life. With Christ in her life, she could be changed. She could handle that debris from a different perspective!

I do struggle with the "debris" of life, just as the caterpillar struggled with the twigs and leaves. With Christ in my life, I am changed, just as the caterpillar becomes a butterfly. I can get over the problems. The message is not that the problems disappear or never occur in the first place. The message is that my perspective is different because I am changed. I can now get over the debris and get on with life!

I remember something Kile observed once. After Terry's death we had several difficult years. We were not only dealing with our sense of loss, but as a family we endured a couple of other real tragedies. One day Kile said, "It seems like life is like a road. You go along for a while and then it gets bumpy, then smooth, then bumpy again."

I think life really is like that. Paul was saying that it's not the bumps in the road or the changes in life that make a difference in us, but how we let Christ change us that makes all the difference.

When I had to face Terry's illness and his death, I needed that difference in myself. Until that time I don't think my understanding of being a Christian went much farther than trying to be a "good" person and to be active in the church. I thought that by my doing "good things" God was smiling on me and, therefore, life was good. Our wonderful life was my reward for being a "good Christian".

While the elements of that thinking were true; I *was* trying to be a Christian, God *was* smiling on me, and life *was* good; that kind of thinking doesn't hold up as well when the bumps in the road of life come into play.

When Terry first became ill I went over and over in my mind all the wrongs I had ever done. What was it I had done that made God send this terrible sorrow our way? Did we need a lesson to learn to appreciate each other in our family? No, we loved each other and we showed it. Did I take our good life for granted? Probably, but surely that wasn't bad enough to justify Terry's death sentence. What had I done wrong?

I came to believe, and still believe to this day, that it was not that God reached out and zapped Terry with leukemia, thus changing our lives forever, because of something we had done or left undone. In believing that, I also had to come to believe that it wasn't our leading a good Christian life that had kept us safe and happy all those years before. A new understanding of grace—that beautiful, gifting word—came to me.

I know now that God didn't sprinkle pixie dust on us so we could have a wonderful life as a reward for doing all the right things. What's more important is that I know God did send His Son to walk through our lives with us so there is nothing in life that can defeat us.

Paul knew that, too. He said, "We are often troubled, but not crushed; sometimes in doubt, but never in despair; there are many enemies, but we are never without a friend; and though badly hurt at times, we are not destroyed" (2 Corinthians 4:8,9).

The other night I got up in the dark to go to the bathroom. I was confident that I knew the way without turning on the light. Suddenly, I tripped over a shoe and lunged forward, banging my head on the door that was only slightly open. If I had put the light on first, I would have easily stepped over the shoe and pushed the door fully open to go through. Sometimes, it seems as though I deal with life that way. I know the difference Christ makes in my life. It's as if I'm walking in the Light. Obstacles are still there, but I can get past them, yet there are times I still neglect to put myself in the Light. I think I can find the way on my own. Those are the times I trip and bang my head.

Christ does make a difference in my life. I used to think the difference was that life would be good. Now I know that's not necessarily true. Life will simply be . . . life. But I will be different—and that's even better.

Many years ago I attended a women's meeting and the speaker said something that I thought was so important I jotted it down and have kept it ever since. She said, "Faith can sing. Pessimism can only cry." When I come upon those bumps in the road of life now, I know I don't have to give in to pessimism and only cry. My faith has taught me that there is still something to sing about.

I read the following prayer the other day. It is attributed only to "an anonymous Confederate soldier."

> I asked God for strength, that I might achieve,
> I was made weak, that I might learn humbly to obey.
> I asked for health, that I might do greater things,
> I was given infirmity, that I might do better things.
> I asked for riches, that I might be happy,
> I was given poverty, that I might be wise.
> I asked for power that I might have the praise of men,
> I was given weakness that I might feel the need of God.
> I asked for all things, that I might enjoy life,
> I was given life, that I might enjoy all things.
> I got nothing that I asked for, but everything that I had hoped for.
> Almost despite myself, my unspoken prayers were answered.
> I am, among all men, most richly blessed.

I was like that soldier when I found that life wasn't turning out the way I asked. I found, as he did, that God touched my life in a way more powerful than I had ever dreamed.

On the back of a torn envelope I found these words I had written down from a sermon I heard long ago. "Our question will not be Job's question, 'God, why are you doing this to me?' but rather 'God, see what is happening to me. Can you help me?' We will turn to God, not to be judged or forgiven, not to be rewarded or punished, but to be strengthened and comforted." God is in control, and we can latch on to that so that it won't really matter what is going on in our lives. We won't need pixie dust to deal with life. All we really need is to place our hand in God's and walk with Him.

I don't wish for pixie dust anymore. It just clouds my vision anyway. What I do wish for, and pray for, is to focus on the Christ that changes me. Even me.
And that does make all the difference.

Questions for Consideration

1. Do you feel that God has blessed your life? Why or why not?

2. Do you think that your good works "earn" you something?

3. Do you think that God causes bad things to happen to us, perhaps to strengthen us or to teach us something?

4. What would you say to someone who has lost a child?

5. What kind of difference does being a Christian actually make in our lives?

Chapter 7

Walking through the Valley

THE VALLEY

It is Monday night—Scout night. He is so weak that I suggest he stay home, but it is his first night as a Webelo Scout and he has been elected Denner. He is so proud of that. He says, "Mom, this is probably the last time in my life that I can go to Scouts. I want to go."

We have not told him the end is probably near, but he seems to know, and to that end he reaches for abundant life, Lord. I will not deny him that.

His father takes him to Scouts.

❖ ❖ ❖

We start the journey to St. Jude's on Tuesday. His father had to carry him on the plane this morning; he was too weak to walk. I know my husband's heart is breaking and I guess it shows on his face. Our boy looks up and says, "Don't cry, Dad."

Oh, Lord, I hurt for all of us! How can we get through this time of sadness?

❖ ❖ ❖

I have been with him every moment. I could not have withstood it any other way because I would have always wondered if he had called out for me. I have to be there.

He was awake all night, Lord, and he asked me about death. He wondered what I thought happened when a person died. He said he was tired of the struggle and the difficult treatments. I told him that his father and I believed that death was not the end of everything, only the end on this earth. For him, that meant the end of sickness and suffering, so death was not something to be afraid of. I told him we believed we would be with God after our death on earth.

You know what he said, Lord? He said he was glad we understood how he felt.

❖ ❖ ❖

I am numb, Lord. I have to be numb or I couldn't stand it. Our son is dead. I must call his father and tell him it's too late for him to get here.

And today is the seventh birthday of our younger son.

We make arrangements and we are in control, but I know we're not really grasping what has happened.

I guess that is the way it must be.

❖ ❖ ❖

Coming home on the plane I thought the first thing I would do when I got home would be to shut the door to the room where all those never-to-be-used-again things of Terry's would cry out to me. I didn't think I could bear to walk down the hall past his empty room.

A strange thing happened, Lord. Our younger son took my hand and urged me down the hall, past that dreaded room, to show me a truck he had received for his birthday. Somehow, I never got around to shutting that door. Thank you, God, for the life that goes on around me and demands my attention.

❖ ❖ ❖

Since we've arrived home, our friends have surrounded us and we truly feel under girded by their concern. Some don't know what to say. Some say just the right words. It doesn't really matter about the words, does it, Lord? It's the circle of love that we feel. That does make a difference. It doesn't seem possible, but we are comforted.

Is that a kind of miracle, Lord? I think it is.

Thank you for that circle of love.

❖ ❖ ❖

We're having a memorial service at our church for our son, and the church is full. I'm glad, Lord. I never realized it before, but it's important to see that people care enough to come to the funeral. It tells me that his life counted with others, too, and we need to know that.

As I listen to the age-old words of comfort I want to say, "Yes, that's really true. It's all right," but the sadness is there for us. To know we can never again share a walk with him in the woods and hills. . . . the grief is there for ourselves.

❖ ❖ ❖

I sit by the graveside as the brief service for the family ends. I feel the touch of a breeze in my hair. I wish everyone would leave so I could be alone in this place to say good-bye. But they all sit waiting for me—just one minute more. I have to KNOW this place. I have to remember exactly what it looks like. That big evergreen tree in front of us; that's good. He would like that.
I can't put it off any longer. I must get up and go on.
Lord, help me to go on.

❖ ❖ ❖

I sensed Terry's presence nearby, Lord. In my mind's eye he was running across a field to the woods on the other side. He stopped and turned towards me, as if I had called to him. He smiled that beautiful smile of his and hesitated, as though waiting for my permission to go on. I nod my head. He turns, in joy, and goes running on.
That's the way it should be, Lord, but I still must face the terrible, overwhelming loneliness inside me.

❖ ❖ ❖

The Mountain

I was brought up to believe that if you wanted to know how to do anything, all you had to do was find a book about it. I believe in the power of the printed page. There are books that will tell us about anything we need to know.

And yet . . . and yet, as I dealt with Terry's death I felt so absolutely lost; I was alone with no guidelines. What was I to do? How was I to act in the face of this totally unbelievable and unacceptable situation?

It is unlikely that any of us will get through life without being touched by the death of someone close to us. I think there are certain lessons we learned on our journey through that particular valley that might help someone else along the way.

Now there are dozens more books about dealing with death than there were when Terry died. Even so, I think if I had to deal with it now, even with all the books, I would still have that sense of being lost, of not knowing exactly what to feel, or say, or do. I think we just have to go with it moment by moment, to just let ourselves be, and do, and say, whatever it is we, as individuals, need to be or do or say at that given moment.

No one can tell us what is the right thing to be experiencing. This is a time when our uniqueness comes into play. So, unlike in other situations, we can't really find the guidelines, or the "how-to" instructions upon which we might rely.

The books about death and dying do have their place, and it is an important one. As we face the death of a loved one, or even our own death, we need to know about those things we should do, that unfinished business that we need to attend to.

After we have lost someone dear to us, the books help us to know the variety of feelings and stages we'll go through. Even though we'll all go through these stages in different ways and on different time schedules, still it is helpful to recognize a stage as we deal with it.

I think that is the single most helpful aspect of the books dealing with death and dying. Knowing that an emotion with which we are dealing is part of grieving helps keep us from adding even more difficulties to the complexity of grief. The most obvious example is when we are dealing with anger. Perhaps I've been going through denial, but now I'm feeling this anger. I really feel angry with the person for leaving me and turning my world upside down. If I can come to understand that this is simply a "normal" part of the healing process, then I don't have to deal with the added burden of feeling guilt over my anger. The grief process is difficult enough without adding unnecessary guilt to it.

Another very helpful aspect of the influx of books on death and dying is that they help teach us what to say or not say to those in grief. This is an area in which I learned a lot as I tried to come to grips with Terry's death. The first thing I learned in the hours and days after I stood by in helpless anguish as Terry's breathing stopped, was that I needed to be with people, people who knew Terry and cared about him.

When I brought Terry to St. Jude for what we knew was the last time, the doctors thought his death would be a gradual thing. They thought he might hang in there for several weeks. For that reason, I brought him there myself, and my husband stayed home in Roanoke with Kile. It was the week of Kile's seventh birthday and he was also going to play in his first ice hockey game. My husband knew that he would be missing days from work as the end for Terry came, so it seemed best for them to wait awhile before they came down to Memphis.

During that last night, though, I could see that things had changed. Terry was so restless; he just couldn't get to sleep.

"Hon, you've just got to try to relax and get some sleep," I told him. "You need to build up your strength."

"Why?" he asked.

"So you'll give the medicines a chance to work and try to get you back in remission," I answered. I still held out that possibility of remission like some golden ring to reach for, but, except for a miracle, I knew there would be no more remissions. He had slipped out of his third remission, and with his rare kind of leukemia, I knew there was no hope. Yet, I couldn't say that to him; I couldn't even say it to myself.

At St. Jude they encourage you to be open and honest about everything: the procedures, the prognoses, everything. The doctors and nurses dealt with the kids and their families that way, and they expected us as parents to do that also. That was the hardest part for us. I think it's just the nature of parents to try and shield their children, and we fell into that in two ways.

First, we could never say to Terry, "You will not be able to live very long with this kind of leukemia. You have, at the best, maybe six months, probably less." We thought we were being honest by agreeing that the doctors said it was a bad kind of leukemia to have, and it was true that people with leukemia have died, but we would quickly add that he could go into remission and then things would be pretty good again.

I remember during one of our many stays at St. Jude a volunteer came into Terry's room to talk to us. She was the mother of a child who had died from leukemia. I know she was trying to be a support person; to see what questions we had and what we needed to talk about with someone who had "been there."

The problem was that I just wasn't ready to face the situation totally. I felt a sense of panic when she came into the room and talked so openly in front of Terry. I didn't want him to even think about children really dying from leukemia. All I could think of was that I had to get her out of there. Maybe her son had died, but mine was doing OK. Mine was surely going to go into remission.

Now, of course, I understand so much more. We needed to get to that point as a family where we could talk about Terry's death as a real possibility. Frank Kile and I talked about it alone in our room toward the end, but not as much as we should have. Neither one of us could bear to bring the other so much pain. There is something I would do differently if given the opportunity. I would be more open in dealing with the very real probability of Terry's death.

The second thing involved Kile. Kile was so young during Terry's illness that we felt it was important to keep his life as normal as possible. While that is good to a point, we should have involved him more in knowing what it was all about. He knew Terry had leukemia, but we assured Kile that when Terry was in remission he would be fine.

Once, when it was necessary for Terry to be an in-patient at St. Jude, we were all in Memphis. We were eating lunch in the hospital cafeteria when Kile asked, "If Terry dies can I get his toys?"

We thought we were handling the question well by not being horrified and by realizing that it was a normal question for a six year old. We could have used that as an opportunity to talk about the possibility of Terry's death. We should have, I think, but we didn't.

"Terry's making progress toward remission," I told Kile. "He'll be fine when he goes into remission."

The day came when Terry was not fine, and could never be fine again. Then what could we tell Kile? Unfortunately, it was a terribly bewildering time for him. We had thought we would have a little time to prepare him, but we wanted to wait until after his birthday. At least let him have a nice birthday, we told ourselves.

Terry died at 8:33 a.m. on the morning of Kile's birthday.
Around 8 a.m. Dr. Simone had said Terry was failing fast. I called my husband and told him to get Kile from school and fly to Memphis as soon as he could.
Then, suddenly, it was too late.
Dr. Simone took me into his office and the secretary dialed our number. As the phone rang I wondered, "What do I say? How can I possibly break the news to Frank Kile that Terry has died? I can't say those words to him."
When he answered, I said, "Hon, it's. . . . you don't need to come down after all."
"What?"
"It's . . . it's too late. Terry died." I felt as though my throat were being torn apart, it was so hard to say those words. I was sobbing by then and on the other end of the telephone, so was Frank Kile.
Years later, Kile told me how he heard his dad answer the phone, and then begin sobbing. "It was the most terrifying thing. I couldn't imagine what was happening," he said.
We could have made that situation a little less terrifying for him if we had talked a little more openly about death. I wish we had. I think Kile understands now that we did the best we could at that time, that we meant to do the best thing for him. We understand, too. We've forgiven ourselves so that we can move on, but still, I wish we'd talked more.
Right from that first moment at Terry's bedside I felt that important sense of support from others. The nurses and Dr. Simone stood with me and let me say good-bye to Terry, then they took me to the office and sat with me as I made my phone calls.

Even more, they continued to sit with me and let me talk about Terry. I told them about when Terry had been born at Camp Pendleton, California, about Frank Kile being out at sea on maneuvers, then three days later they flew him back by helicopter when they got close enough for the helicopter to reach land. The helicopter set down in front of the Naval Hospital and Frank Kile strode in wearing his field uniform, just as Terry and I were leaving the hospital. He was able to spend about fifteen minutes with us. I told them how funny it looked to see this tiny new baby being held by this man in a combat uniform.

I told them about our first trip to St. Jude when we thought maybe Terry didn't really have leukemia and then how we thought he might be one of the lucky ones and stay in remission. I told them how it just didn't seem right. Terry was such a wonderful, bright, beautiful child who could have made the world a better place. It just wasn't right.

Finally, I fell silent. They continued to sit with me. I just shook my head. I couldn't find the words. I wanted to scream out, but I didn't know what to scream. I looked at Dr. Simone. Clenching my fists, I cried out, "I hate this! I HATE this!!"

He sat looking at me as he said softly, "So do we."

Soon our dear friends, Joe and Margaret Wilson, arrived from their home across the river in Marion, Arkansas and took me to their home. I had not slept for several days, and they put me to bed until it was time for Frank Kile and Kile to arrive.

Once there, Frank Kile made the arrangements with the funeral home, and in the early dawn the three of us flew back home to Roanoke. We changed planes in Birmingham, Alabama and went into the coffee shop for some coffee. I had never noticed before, but tables are set with FOUR chairs. The empty chair at our table seemed to cry out to me in my sadness.

In Roanoke, as we dragged ourselves off the plane to face the day, we were surprised to find Ed Ridout, our minister and friend, there. He did not know when we would be returning. He had just planned to meet every plane until we got home. From that moment, the feeling of being under girded, of being held up when you can't hold yourself up, began for us.

Today if someone were facing the death of a loved one and asked me, "How can I bear it?" I would have to shake my head and say, "I don't know." I don't know exactly what mechanics of life got us through those first days, but I know that somehow, moment-by-moment, life went on and we went on with it.

As human beings we know that life on this earth is finite. We know that people die, that tragedies occur, that terrible situations can happen to us. As Christians, we know there is a loving and powerful God who is with us, yet even knowing all that, when the loss and tragedy involve us and our loved ones, there is a huge gap between taking what we know and absorbing it into our hearts to give us peace.

We feel as though a terrible physical blow has struck us; we reel against it, almost gasping for breath. I can remember my first reaction when, a few years ago, I got the word that my mother had collapsed with an aneurysm and was dying.

"NO!" I remember yelling from a place deep inside me. "No!"

Life hits us with situations from which the very fiber of our being yells, "No!" We wish it weren't so for us. We wish it weren't so for our friends when we see it happening to them, but it happens. What do we do when it does happen? What CAN we do to get to that place where we can again affirm the Yes! of life?

When Terry died Kile asked, "Will we ever be happy again?" I really wondered that myself, but I answered, "Yes. There will always be a part of us that misses Terry, but we will be happy again." It has been true.

Finding the affirmations of life again began for us, I think, at that time when we arrived at the airport to find someone there for us. After we got home, all through that day and the next few days our friends came by. That meant so much.

I had always been a person who shied away from going to visit someone with a recent loss. I never knew what to say, and I thought they'd probably rather be alone anyway. Now, I understand that it's not the words our friends said that mattered. Today I couldn't tell you one thing anyone said to us with their words, but I can tell you what they said to me by coming to see me. They told us that we mattered to them. They acknowledged that Terry's life meant something, and therefore his death meant loss. That's all we really needed to hear.

We had a memorial service at our church on Sunday afternoon. The church was full, and that meant a lot to us. Again, I felt the voice of our congregation and friends and people from Terry and Kile's school saying that we mattered to them. I think that is one of those important "bottom lines" of life, knowing that who we are and what we do matters.

We filed in and took our place in the front pew with our family and my close friend, Ann Jester. I watched as Scott Ridout, Ed and Merle's son, came down the aisle as an acolyte to light the candles. He and Terry had been best friends, as his parents were to us and his brother, Steve was to Kile. Scott and Terry had served as acolytes together so many times, and seeing Scott walking down the aisle all alone was heart breaking. Scott lit the candles, then turned and walked to the empty pew opposite us and sat down. I wanted to go over to him and gather him in my arms. I wanted to bring him over to sit with us so he wouldn't be alone, but I didn't. I just sat there knowing that the pain of loss was washing over all of us.

Ed's sermon was a wonderful affirmation of Terry's life. He began by saying, "The length of one's life has no bearing on its meaning." The meaning, he explained, came from the way we live the moments that we do have:

> The real tragedy is not when a task is left unfinished by a worker who has been called away, but when a task was never begun at all. . . . The personal tragedy, the waste, lies in what we can do with time and do not; the love we do not give; the effort we do not make; the power we do not use; the happiness we do not earn; the kindnesses we neglect to bestow; the gratitude we have not expressed; the noble thoughts and deeds that could be ours only if we would realize why we are here.

Ed reminded us of how Terry always reached for that fuller life no matter what his struggles were. He talked about Terry's Scout work, his golfing, and his trying to keep up with the kids in the neighborhood. He had hung in there. Ed reminded us that even during Terry's last days he was still trying to keep up with his schoolwork. He was too weak to sit up and write the answers, so he said to his homebound teacher, "I'll just tell you the answers if you'll write them for me." He didn't say, "I can't do this. I quit." He never said, "I quit. I can't." Ever. Ed held up Terry's courage and inner strength as a model for us to remember. That, too, said to us that Terry's life mattered, made a difference, counted for something.

Later in the service our choir director sang a solo of *How Great Thou Art*.[1] It is such a beautiful, powerful hymn. The words touched me as no other hymn could have, but it was a long, long time after that before I again could sing that hymn without tears.

The next day, Monday, we flew with our family and Ed Ridout to Memphis, where we had a graveside service for Terry, and he was laid to rest at Memphis Memorial Gardens.

It was a beautiful, clear day, but it was a terrible day, too. We had insisted that we wanted to keep the coffin closed, not to see Terry as he was now. I had my final goodbye at St. Jude, and Frank Kile simply did not want to see Terry dead. Ed tried to encourage us to have a last goodbye, but we were adamant. Now, I think we were wrong.

If I had it to do over again, I would have those last few minutes with Terry. I had seen him at the time of death, but my husband had not. I think we needed to do that, painful as it might have been. I think there must be some inexplicable thread in the tapestry of grief that makes having to acknowledge the death as a reality, face to face, a first step toward healing the pain.

We had a short service at the graveside and then, suddenly, it was over. Somehow, everyone seemed ready to go on, but I wasn't ready to go on. I knew that once I got up from my seat and we made our way out of the cemetery, it was the turning point that would really mark the end of my dealing with Terry's life. From that moment on, I would only be dealing with his death. I wasn't ready for that. I wanted to stay there. I wanted time to stand still.

I sensed that everyone was waiting for me to get up. I really wished they would all leave. I wanted to be left there alone with Terry to say good-bye, to say all those things I'd meant to say to him . . . someday. I did not want to have to get up and go on with life.

It says in the Scriptures that man is wonderfully made, and time and again I marvel at the truth of that. God seems to have put into us something that reaches for life, even when we are so numb with despair we cannot feel ourselves reaching. It was that something inside me, I think, that finally gave me the strength to get up from my seat at that grave side and go on. By taking those first few steps, I was beginning the journey. I could not sit by the graveside forever. It was time to move on.

When Terry first became ill, I felt that we were at the beginning, the beginning of looking at our life and dealing with it in a whole new way. When Terry died, there was no doubt in my mind that it was the ending.

With those first reluctant steps away from Terry's grave, I was not simply continuing with "the ending." I had reached the point toward which I had been heading from the very first day. It was time for beginning again. It was time to walk again into the affirmation of life, the Yes! that must come in the face of every No! I did not think about it in any conscious way at the time, but it was there nevertheless.

It would not happen easily.

But it WOULD happen!

QUESTIONS FOR CONSIDERATION

1. What part does our church community play in dealing with a death?

2. What is an individual Christian's responsibility when someone dies?

3. What should a Christian's approach be when the loved one of a non-Christian dies?

4. What do you remember most about a time when you dealt with the death of someone close to you?

5. If you knew you were approaching your own death, how would you want people to relate to you?

Chapter 8
"...And the Other Is Wings"

THE VALLEY

As the pain of sadness eases I am beginning to realize how intense it has been. I am realizing that I have felt an actual pain inside, in my heart and in my throat. The tears come so easily. Sometimes, my arm literally *aches* to go around Terry's shoulder again.

I know I must let this grief come, Lord. I cannot keep it inside or it will grow like a cancer. Help me, Lord, to handle this grief. Thank you for the friends who will listen to my heartache.

❖ ❖ ❖

We went to an amusement park today, Lord. A day of fun, but the sadness is there inside. I looked into the faces of other people, wondering what their burden is.

And I looked for Terry, Lord, wanting . . . WILLING him to be there, but he wasn't.

There was a boy with blonde hair, but no, it wasn't he. There was a tall and lanky boy, but no, not Terry either—nor was the boy with the same plaid slacks that Terry owned—nor any of the others. I looked at them, knowing I was foolish, but I couldn't help it. I wished—how hard I wished—that one of them could have been Terry. It was almost as if I wanted to trick myself into believing he was there.

I can't really do that, Lord, and I guess that's a good thing.

Those boys who reminded me of Terry weren't really like him at all. I was made aware, again, of his uniqueness, of the uniqueness of every one of your children, Father-of-us-all. What a gift you gave us in that. How special each person is in their own individual way, and how wonderful to know someone well enough to recognize that uniqueness.

The sadness has passed, Lord. Thank you for the day.

❖ ❖ ❖

Last week, as I was repainting Terry's old room, a friend said to me, "Don't torment yourself by thinking of the suffering at the end." I didn't understand what she meant because that was the reason I could let him go, to end his suffering.

Now I understand, Lord. I guess the numbness is wearing off and we have to face the full reality. Suddenly, I remembered the end, and the horror washed over me, leaving me limp.

I am beginning to realize that there are memories, fears, sorrows that we must face slowly, as we can, and we must come to terms with them.

Help me, Lord.

❖ ❖ ❖

"... And the Other Is Wings"

The transfers and moves that my husband's job brings us, Lord, usually excite me, but this time it's different. I don't want to move to a place where no one knows who Terry was, to a house that will never know his footfall. I feel like we're leaving him behind us, Lord, and I can't really let him go that easily. My husband is glad to be leaving this home. It is painful for him to be among so many reminders, but they comfort me.

I know that whatever our feelings might be, we have to go on with this move, Lord, and we have to go on with life. We will pray for your help and strength as we did in the beginning, and at the ending, and now in our beginning again.

We will go on with life.

❖ ❖ ❖

The Mountain

Letting go. I think learning to do that is one of life's most poignant lessons. We understand that it is a goal for us with our children. We must let go to the extent that they can become mature, independent adults. The process begins at the moment of their birth.

My sister-in-law cross-stitched a wonderful saying for us many Christmases ago. It says, "You can give your children two gifts; one is roots; the other is wings." We, as parents, don't seem to have as much trouble with the roots as we do with the wings.

We're familiar with the story of the prodigal son found in Luke 15:11–32. There are so many lessons found in this parable and preachers have preached on them for generations. To me, though, one of the important lessons in this Scripture has spoken to my heart in recent years. It concerns the message about the father letting the son go, letting the son be free to experience life as a result of his own choices.

When the day came that the son went to his father and said, "I want my part of the inheritance. I want to be free to go," there is no doubt in my mind that the father wanted to say, "Wait. Think about this a little longer. You have everything you need here," but the father didn't do that. He knew an important truth. He understood that our children will not be all they can be, will not be what God intends for them to be, while remaining under our care and protection. They have to be free enough to experience the trials and triumphs of life so that they know who they are and of what they are made. Because the father loved the son, he had no choice. He had to let him go. It was time.

That is a difficult lesson for us, as parents, to learn. I remember when Terry first began learning to ride a two-wheeler. We were living out on a farm in Missouri where the space for trying new things spread out from our doorstep through lawn and pastures. Terry would mount his bike as I held it steady. As he set his grip with determination, I would begin pushing faster and faster until, with a final thrust, he went forward . . . and crashed. Again and again we went through the ordeal. Each time, as he picked himself up he would say, "I think I'm getting it. Let's try one more time." When his dad was home, he would work with Terry. By this time Terry had begun wearing his football pads. It was a painful procedure, but, finally, the day came when he kept going! He did not crash. Peddling furiously, he went all the way across our lawn and into the field. We cheered and jumped up and down in our excitement. He had done it! What a victory. What a lesson for life. It was a difficult thing to do as a parent, to let go of that bike, knowing he would crash, but if we hadn't done that, he would never have had the victory.

We're facing another time of letting go as I write this. Our younger son, Joel will graduate from college in May. Although he has not been at home for four years, including summers when he worked in Nebraska and Michigan, there is a strange finality in having the last of our children be completely on their own. I do not think he will "crash." I fully expect him to "keep peddling," yet, I am aware that there is a sense of letting go inside me with which I must deal. But, it is time.

The understanding of timing is important. I've learned over the years that there are a myriad ways of letting go as our boys were growing up. We would not have turned them loose on a two-wheeled bike when they were too young to master that riding skill. We needed to be aware of the timing of many skill levels.

During the entire senior year of Kile's high school career, I can remember that I felt like crying every time I thought of our first child going off to college. It didn't help that he kept teasing me by saying, "Just think, Mom, this is the LAST time we'll be able to do this . . ." I just wasn't ready for that time. I wondered if he were ready, but when the day came that we helped him move into the dormitory at the University of New Mexico, I knew the time was right. I knew he was ready, so I felt at peace about it. That is not to say I didn't miss him, didn't worry about him, didn't wish he weren't so far away from Birmingham, Alabama where we were living. I still knew the time was right for him to make this step. Like the father of the prodigal son, there was no real choice. It was time.

When each of our boys was born I prayerfully placed them into God's hands. When Terry became ill and died, I had serious second thoughts about doing that. Why should I give my boys to God if He was going to take them away from me in such a terrible way? My placing them in God's hands was supposed to keep them safe. It was like a special insurance policy.

I said at the time of their birth, that I understood our children are not ours to own or to keep forever as our possessions. I understood that they were loaned to us for a time to enrich our lives as we nurtured theirs. I said I understood that, but I didn't really. I didn't understand what that concept meant in the face of giving up a child to death.

I was prepared to let go of a bicycle to let my children learn to ride. I was prepared to let go as they went to school to learn and develop their potential. I was prepared to let them go as they drove off in the family car that first time, or married, or began their families. I was not prepared to let go of their earthly reality in such a final way that I could not call them on the phone, or write to them, or touch their lives in some way. It never occurred to me that I would have to do that.

Even now, I don't think there is a way we can really prepare for that kind of letting go and I don't think God expects us to. At the same time, I think each of us can become the kind of person who will not let that absolute kind of letting go destroy us. I think God wants that for us.

I have come to believe that it is important to have the understanding that our children are not ours to own. Combined with this is the belief that God wants us to be the best we can be, to develop to the maximum of our potential. We cannot do this, and our children cannot do this, when we are not free to experience life. I think this is the first lesson God wants us to learn about letting go. In the "normal" course of life it is a good and natural thing. In the "exceptional" course, in the absolute, final letting go of a child to death God is there with us to help us handle it.

There are other areas of life in which "letting go" is an important lesson. The second area in which I think God is nudging us to let go is when those experiences and memories of our past are interfering with our living of today.

There is so much material out these days about how important it is to "heal the inner child" that exists within each of us. In a recent parenting series our adult Sunday school class studied, we learned that the first step for us to be good parents involved understanding ourselves. This included the concept that we all have what the study authors called "wounded memories," those painful things from the past that still influence the way we act today. We all carry unnecessary baggage from the past. What we need to do is consider whether or not the weight of it is slowing us down.

A lot of the burdens from the past come from the way we perceive our relationship with our parents. One of the books I found most helpful in considering this issue is *The Blessing* by Gary Smalley and John Trent. They acknowledge the importance of sensing the parent has bestowed "the blessing" on the child as was done in ancient days. They further deal with the fact that unless we have cleared up that relationship we will have trouble with any other relationships.

They say, "Only when we can honestly look at our parents and our past are we ever truly free to 'leave' them in a healthy way and 'cleave' to others in present relationships. (Genesis 2:24) If we are carrying around anger or resentment from the past, we are not free to 'leave'. Rather, we are chained to the past and are likely to repeat it."[1]

As I look back on my own childhood I have so many memories, some good, some not. There are some of those not-so-good memories that I have needed to release, yet I think the process of letting go involves more than just saying "I'm putting these memories behind me and getting rid of them forever." I don't think I can really do that until I take them out, examine them for what they were and then I am able to leave them behind.

One of my favorite Scriptures has always been Matthew 11:28 (KJV), "Come unto me, all who labor and are heavy-laden, and I will give you rest." When I hear those words of comfort before Communion I almost feel the physical sensation of taking a heavy load off my shoulders and setting it down at the foot of the cross. Then comes that sigh of relief.

Our minister once said in a sermon, "We can't fix our yesterdays." We all know that's probably true, yet we seem to keep working at it. I have found myself taking out hurtful memories from the past like a dog might take out an old bone that it can't leave buried, and I keep gnawing away at them. These hurtful memories involve things that have happened in the past. They are over. It's time to leave them behind.

The next step after putting away hurtful memories is often reconciliation. I believe in reconciliation. Behind our home in New Mexico we have a beautiful tree. Something happened to it a long time ago to cause the trunk to separate about eight feet up into two distinct trunks and grow curving away from each other. Further up, it curves back together and the branches appear to be hugging each other. I call it The Reconciliation Tree.

We can be like that tree. Even if there are things that divided us at one time, we can learn to come back together and embrace each other. This can happen when we let go of hurtful memories.

Finally, I think, God has touched my heart in such a way that I have a real sense of the fact that with Him we really can let go of those things we need to put behind us. Where else but at God's feet can we dump the debris of life? I can come to Him with those painful childhood memories, those present-day frustrations and discouragement, those sticks and stones of life that do hurt. I can drop them down right there, but even better, I can walk away and leave them there. I know that He will never bring them up again and thrust them in my face. I can put them behind me forever.

There is a third area of life that I have learned I need to let go: the busy-ness of life. It seems we are so programmed to stay busy that we have forgotten the wonderful blessing of being still.

God tries to remind us of the importance of quietude through Scriptures and hymns. "Be still and know that I am God" (Psalm 46:10), He says to us. That old hymn, *Be Still My Soul*,[2] reminds us that if we are calm and quiet so we can hear our God, we will find the strength and comfort for which we are searching.

I just finished talking with a young mother on the phone. She works outside the home, has a busy young family, and is involved in her community. "Am I the only one who can't do it all?" She asked this in frustration as she went on to enumerate the many pulls on her life. "I never have a minute for ME!" she exclaimed. "I can never even read a book." I listened with sympathy because I know the very real pressures with which she is dealing. That is the way it is for so many Americans today. If that is so, when do we have time to be still and know God?

If I can never take the time for quietness, how can I talk to God? How can I hear Him in order to understand how He might guide my life? If He isn't able to guide my life, where am I going anyway?

I have found that when I don't let go of the busy-ness I not only don't have time for God or for me, but I also don't have time for my husband and children. It is too easy to lose those relationships that are most important to us in the shuffle of busy activities.

Years ago I cut the following poem out of a magazine. It is yellowing with age, but it is still meaningful for me.

Timing

There are so many distractions
(Turn down the TV; turn down the world),
So many people
(Guess who called today? What's doing tomorrow?)
So much glitz, gloss, glimmer, glitter
That it's hard for marriage
To end up
With anything but
A dull finish,
Unless, of course,
Along the way
You are one of those
Who takes the time
To take time. (author unknown)

I'm learning that along the way I have to take the time for God, for myself, and for those relationships I cherish. To do this I have to let go of those things that clutter my life with busy-ness.

Letting go. Yes, it's an important concept. We have to learn how to let go in some cases, as with our children.

"...And the Other Is Wings"

Sometimes we have to learn what it is we need to let go, as with hurtful memories, or busyness. Much of letting go has to do with the timing.

Maybe life is like a dance. As we glide through life we try to hear the beat and keep time to it. Our arms swing around as we circle and dip, sometimes enfolding as we might hug something to us, and sometimes sweeping wide open as we might let something go.

I guess it's all in the timing.

QUESTIONS FOR CONSIDERATION

1. How involved should parents be with their child as that child grows to adulthood?

2. As an adult, how have you come to understand your relationship with your parents?

3. What is the most important thing we can give our children?

4. What are some things you might need to let go of?

5. How can we change the busy-ness of American life? Do we want to?

CHAPTER 9

Like a Rock—What It Means to Trust God

THE VALLEY

Today I helped with an outing for severely retarded children. I could hardly get through the day, Lord. First, I thought of the sadness the parents must have felt upon first learning that their children could never realize the dreams the parents might have for them.
Then—this is the worst part; I hope you'll understand and forgive—I looked at the ones who couldn't walk or talk or sit up and who cried and cried in their misery, and I thought, why couldn't one of these have died in place of our son? They seem so miserable. He was so bright, so interested in everything. He was compassionate. He cared so much about this earth; he could have made a better world. Why him, Lord?
 I have to come to terms with that and it isn't easy. I know there isn't a logical answer. I find comfort in the idea that we're looking at the underside of a tapestry. The design does not

make sense to us, but from the other side—from Your view—we would see the beautiful and complete picture.
I guess I will simply have to trust you, Lord. I can do that . . . most of the time.

❖ ❖ ❖

There is something that troubles me. When I hear someone telling about Your healing hand curing another, I am angry. Do they imply that their loved one had more faith than we did? Or do they imply that their loved one was worth more than Terry?
No, I guess that deep down they don't mean any of those things. My anger is simply because I want it to have been our Terry, our own son that we miss so much, to have been the one to feel Your healing touch.
I know You could have done it, Lord, if it had been the best thing, and in this life, I'll never understand why it wasn't.
When our younger son asked in anguish, "Why didn't God answer our prayers and make Terry well?" I finally was able to answer that You had answered our prayers because his brother was no longer sick and hurting, but was well again. You just didn't answer our prayers the way we wanted.
Maybe when I can fully accept that myself I will find peace.

❖ ❖ ❖

THE MOUNTAIN

Trusting God. It sounds so simple, but the issue is how can we get to that place where we can really put our trust in God? For me, there are times in my life when I do that, then I snatch back a little area of my life for ME to control.

The Scriptures are full of words encouraging us to be trusting. Psalm after psalm praises a God we can trust, no matter what the despair.

Psalm 12, verse 6, tells us, "The promises of the Lord can be trusted: they are as genuine as silver refined seven times in the furnace." Of course, seven refers to the number of perfection, completeness.

The psalmist cries in Psalm 56, verses 3 and 4, "When I am afraid, O Lord Almighty, I put my trust in You. I trust in God and am not afraid: I praise Him for what He has promised. What can a mere human being do to me?"

As I look back over the experiences of my life, it surprised me to realize that it was easier for me to trust God during the difficult times. When I've had problems and concerns, perhaps because I can't fix them myself, it is easier for me to turn to God and say, "Now YOU fix it!" When life is easy and good though, it's as if I say, "Look how well I am handling things." I am more apt to believe and trust in my own abilities and myself rather than in God.

So, how do I learn to trust in God?

I think it is similar to my relationships with people. There is a parallel between how we come to trust others and how we come to trust God.

We have moved a lot in our married life. When we moved to our present home in Virginia, it was our sixteenth move in our thirty-eight years of marriage. At each new place there is a period of time before I make a real friend, a person I can talk with heart-to-heart and share with, a person I can trust. It's impossible to meet someone and immediately have that feeling of enough trust that I can share my inner self, my thoughts and feelings. I first must get to know that person. I believe the same is true of my relationship with God. I have to come to know Him before I can trust Him.

The real question is, how can I come to know God? For me, it is through study and worship, through Sunday school and sharing. It is through reading the Word and having a quiet time for reflection. It is through being open to possibilities, living with the expectation of God's presence through the living Christ in my life.

This relationship doesn't come without time and effort on my part, just as a new friendship will not develop without time and effort on my part. I have to focus on the God I have come to know through Christ.

E. Stanley Jones was a giant in the field of teaching us how to be close to God. He wrote something at the age of eighty-eight as he was recovering from a stroke that has meant a great deal to me. He wrote, "I'm happy because my happiness isn't based on happiness. It's based on Him." (Jesus)

This says to me that there is a special kind of joy for us when we focus on the Christ, and that this joy can supersede anything that is going on in our lives. For E. Stanley Jones this meant even physical problems, such as a stroke. When I have that special relationship with Christ, I can trust in God that nothing will defeat me, but I need to have the relationship before the trust can be there.

When he was about six years old, our youngest son Joel taught me how important that trust is. At that time we were vacationing on the gulf coast of Alabama. The day had started out sunny and calm, but had changed slowly so that by late afternoon it was windy and rough.

Even so, my husband and our two sons, Kile, then sixteen years old, and Joel, wanted to experience riding in a catamaran, a two-hulled, outrigger type of boat with a sail.

They had signed up to ride early in the day, but there was a long list of people ahead of them. By the time it was finally their turn, I was concerned about the roughness of the water. Even Jim (not his real name), the manager of the ride, didn't want to fight the waves any more, but he found another young man who agreed to take them out.

While they were gone I sat on the beach, reading and dozing. Glancing at my watch at 4:45 I thought they should be almost back, but there was no sight of them. When I looked up the beach to Jim's post, it was not reassuring to see him searching the horizon through his binoculars.

My heart turned icy with fear, but I tried to appear calm as I walked up to him. "What's going on?" I asked.

"Oh, they've tipped over, but they're OK."

"What do you mean? Can you see them?"

"Sure. I can see the side of the cat sitting in the water."

And so, I found myself standing on the Alabama shore staring helplessly at the gulf. We waited and watched, and watched and waited. Another half hour passed.

Finally Jim decided to go in the other catamaran to help them. They evidently couldn't get the boat upright again. Because of the rough water it seemed to take forever for the second catamaran to get headed out.

Jim's young assistant kept watch through the binoculars. Suddenly he exclaimed, "I just can't see them any more!"

I felt an even greater sense of fear as I took the binoculars from him. Searching the horizon I, too, could no longer see any trace of them. I wanted to scream, "Do something! Do something! That's my whole family out there!" I couldn't believe this was happening. A sense of terror surged within me. It isolated me behind a wall of fear that was so great I could scarcely pray.

Thank goodness they had life jackets on! Even so, the idea of my husband and my sons, especially six-year-old Joel, being in that water for over an hour and a half with darkness coming on was more than I could stand. I knew there were sharks out there.

I continued my fearful vigil, trying to pray and fighting my sense of panic. An eternity passed before I saw Jim's catamaran headed back. After an agonizing wait he beached the boat.

"I couldn't get to them, but the cat's upright," Jim reported. "I saw it headed to a beach up shore."

I ran to our van and raced along the beach road, but wasn't able to spot them. I did see a jeep headed back to our area, so I hurried back to that beach.

Suddenly I saw my husband and Joel calmly walking toward me! The tension of my unspoken fears finally broke then, and, surprisingly, anger replaced it.

I stormed up to them, choking on my anger. I sputtered, "Where have you been? What happened? Where's Kile? I knew you shouldn't have gone out there!"

My husband put his arm around me and said, "Everything's all right. The boys are bringing the cat in. They let us off a ways up the beach and the sheriff's car brought us down."

"What happened?" I asked, still trembling.

"We tipped over," reported Joel.

"The boys kept trying to upright the boat, but they drifted way away from us. It was too far to swim to them or to shore, so Joel and I just drifted out there until they finally got the boat upright and came back for us," my husband said.

"You were floating out there for an hour and a half?" I asked incredulously.

"Yeah, and those jelly fish kept stinging us!" exclaimed Joel.

I hugged him tightly. "Weren't you scared?"

"No, Mom, we were OK," he told me. "I just thought about that Jesus storybook you read me. You know. It says God is always with us. I knew God and Jesus would take care of us. I didn't get scared at all."

"That's right," added my husband. "If he had panicked or gotten upset we *would* have had a big problem, but he was just as calm as could be. I was really proud of him!"

Many times since that day I have thought about that . . . a small boy's faith . . . the lesson for me. Mostly what I think about is the simple truth of it: that God was indeed there with Joel and his dad. God had been with me, too, if only I had stopped panicking long enough to remember. Knowing that God is there and relying on him *can* make a difference. It did for Joel. It can for me. It can for you, too.

Over the years I've thought a lot about trusting God, trying to understand how to develop that trust. The first step for me is by knowing God, but I've realized that knowing Him still isn't enough. The second step for me was to simply do it, simply take that step in faith and put my trust in Him. That's the hard part.

A few years ago we watched a cutting horse show for the first time. It was quite something to watch! The contestant and his horse walk slowly through the herd of calves until one is separated, or cut, from the herd. Once separated, the calf tries frantically to rejoin the herd. The horse, darting this way and that, cuts the calf off each time, keeping it separated for a set amount of time.

I was amazed, first of all that the rider could stay in the saddle with such swift, sudden movements in any given direction, and secondly, that such a large animal as a horse could twist and turn and change directions with such speed and agility.

As each horse and rider took his turn, I was able to notice more of the subtleties of the event. I began to see that the key to success was for the rider to let the reins lie loosely and to trust his horse to know which way to dart, rather than for the rider to clue the horse by a pull of the reins. When the rider tried to be the controlling force, he didn't do as well.

I couldn't help but think that this was an analogy to the way I am with God. I have trouble getting to the point of letting go of the reins of my life, so to speak, of not wanting to keep some control.

It is a simple thing to let the reins lay loosely on the cutting horse's neck, but only if the rider first knows and trusts his horse. I noticed that the riders who had less experience with their horses tended to grab up the reins again, and then things would not go as well for them.

In my own life I continue to want to clue God as to how He should move in my life. The more I come to know Him, however, the more I can trust Him. The act of trusting involves my willingness to loosen up on the reins of control of my own life. It is a simple matter to do that, yet it's also a profound step. I simply have to do it. I can't get to that point by reasoning or logic. It is a matter of faith based on experience and knowledge.

The cutting horse rider must get to the point of knowing his horse well enough to know he can count on it. Then he will be able to trust his horse enough to let the reins be loose. I, too, can get to that point in my relationship with God.

From past experiences I now know that if I had trusted God instead of trying to stay in control of things myself, I would have done better. For me, the message of the cutting horse show was "let go and let God." The way to do that is simply to trust Him.

Paul teaches that lesson over and over, by his words and by his life. In Philippians 4:6 he says, "Don't worry about anything, but in all your prayers ask God for what you need, always asking Him with a thankful heart." What a bold statement that is! "Don't worry about anything." How can we possibly do that?

I think it is possible by becoming like little children and simply trusting. Little children, by their very nature, are trusting toward their parents, unless experience has taught them otherwise. They know who loves them and looks out for them. How much more our Father loves us! If I could develop the mindset of a trusting child I could more easily make that leap of faith to a state of trusting God.

I love the reassurance in that old hymn, *Trust and Obey*.[1] The words tell us to "never fear." With all there is to fear in life today, those words carry tremendous comfort. I know now that I can hope to get to the point where I never fear because of the God in whom I can put my trust. There is a responsibility on my part. I must make the effort. I must cross that bridge of faith. I must trust and obey.

Proverbs 3 gives advice to a young man. The entire passage is full of what the young man needs to know. It includes this, "Trust in the Lord with all your heart. Remember the Lord in everything you do, and He will show you the right way" (Proverbs 3:5,6).

A few years ago our family was facing a crossroads as far as my husband's career choices were concerned. Another company was buying his company and he had to decide if he wanted to continue with them or go elsewhere. No matter what the decision, it meant leaving a place we loved and where we wanted to stay. I remember thinking how helpful it would be if we could see ahead and know exactly what the outcome of each possible choice might be.

We felt assured, however, that God could help us in the decision making process, but only because we already had a relationship with Him. We believed that He would show us the "right way" as Proverbs tells us, but first we had to "trust" and "remember the Lord in everything we do." Now, with the benefit of hindsight, we can see that we made the best choice, especially because of where He continued to lead us.

Last year during Lent as we entered the final days of Holy Week, I realized that we have the most powerful example of trust in God when we look at Christ Himself. As He went into that turbulent and terrifying time of betrayal and death, He knew what was to come. Even so, He was able to trust His heavenly Father so completely that He could say, "Not my will, but thine . . ."

Whenever I focus on Christ I am able to learn more about what my relationship to God should be. I am able to learn about the nature of God. I have learned that He is not only strong, but also omnipotent. He is not only there for me during prayer time, but He is omnipresent. He not only knows my heart, but He is omniscient. He is sturdy, reliable, solid, and mighty. I really can trust Him.

He is a rock.

Questions for Consideration

1. Are you a trusting person? Can others trust you?

2. In what areas of your life do you need to trust God more?

3. Can we live with a sense of complete trust in God? How would that affect our lives?

4. How can we learn to trust God?

5. How do we learn to trust each other? Does that affect our ability to trust God?

CHAPTER 10

"O for a Thousand Tongues to Sing"

THE VALLEY

It's Christmas time again and we approach it with mixed emotions. We still carry such grief for our loss, yet through it we are made aware again of the precious gifts of love, friendship, compassion, and joy that are still part of life. We miss Terry so much, but we cannot ignore the blessing of his life. We cannot ignore the blessing—and the joy and enthusiasm—of our younger son's life. We cannot discount the goodness of being together.

This year as we write our Christmas letter we will do as we do each Christmas season. We will take time to pause and look back on the past year, then turn and go forward into the new one with grateful hearts for all we have had, and knowing that our faith and the love of family and friends will continue to give meaning to life.

We said all that in our Christmas letter, Lord, and we really meant it. Thank you that we COULD mean it.

❖ ❖ ❖

Time has taken care of a lot of the hurting, but there are some things that seem to need a conscious effort of will on our part. For a long time now, whenever I am involved in an activity that brings me pleasure, the scene of Terry dying flashes through my mind.

Lord, it seems as if a part of me is saying, "You shouldn't be enjoying yourself. How can you be disloyal to your son that way?" And yet, I know from some inner strength You are giving me that I must get on with life. I must enjoy again.

But I struggle with this.

When I look at all the pictures of Terry I am reassured of the joy in his life by the expressions on his face, even in the picture taken just days before he died. I feel he would not want us to mourn him forever.

And yet, Lord, I STRUGGLE with this!

❖ ❖ ❖

I laughed today, Lord—really laughed. It has been such a long time since I have felt joy. It feels so good to have joy bubbling out in laughter again.

I saw my husband watch me laugh, his face tender and glad that I have come this far from the shadows of sadness. Thank you, Lord, for that touch of joy, and for the strength to have come far enough to feel that touch.

❖ ❖ ❖

On the day of his brother's death our younger son asked, "Will we ever be happy again?" We answered then that we would, but there probably would always be a little place inside us that was sad because we missed his brother.

It has been so.

We have had nice family outings and vacations, and we have been happy, even though the first few times there would always be that moment when we would come together and weep, so saddened were we that we couldn't share this with our older boy. Now, Lord, there is simply a moment when our eyes meet and we share the pain in silent communication.

Does that mean we're growing, Lord?

※ ※ ※

THE MOUNTAIN

If I had been writing this book some years ago I would have stopped before this final chapter. Only in recent years am I coming to realize in my relationship with the Lord the importance of praise and thanksgiving for the joy of life. Whereas before I would approach my prayer time with my supplications, now I try to begin with praise.

There is the reminder of the importance of praise in our Scriptures. Hebrews 13:15 says, "Let us, then, always offer praise to God as our sacrifice through Jesus, which is the offering presented by lips that confess Him as Lord." Further in 1 Peter 4:11, "Whoever preaches must preach God's messages; whoever serves must serve with the strength that God gives him, so that in all things praise may be given to God through Jesus Christ, to whom belong glory and power forever and ever. Amen." In all things praise is to be given to God.

I'm not sure just when the change in my prayer life occurred. It was a gradual thing. When a Bible study I was taking emphasized that prayer should begin with praise, I realized that my heart was ready to do that. I had come past the point of railing against God, past the point of stewing over what might have been. I had come back to the point of knowing that God was always with me as a loving Father. I finally understood that His loving presence required a response from me. That response can only be praise and thanksgiving.

Wanting to praise God was not really a new feeling for me. When I was a young person I had a wonderful fantasy in which I had a beautiful singing voice, which I would use to sing God's praises. This wouldn't have been such an unusual fantasy except that I have what is probably the world's worst singing voice.

I prayed and prayed for a miracle to change my voice into something beautiful. I could even envision the miracle—rays of light would come into the dimly lit church of my childhood. The light would shine on me, transforming me, and my voice would become a pure, rich, beautiful singing voice. Oh, how I would sing! I fully intended to use it for God's glory.

It didn't happen. I would open my mouth to sing praises, but only a croaky noise would come out. I heard the notes in my mind. I knew the music, but I had no control over how it sounded when it came out of my mouth.

I grew up in a very small town. Classes were so small that in Junior High School, everyone was in the chorus. When it came time for the concerts, however, the director always gave me a special job, an excuse to keep me from singing. At the Christmas concert I held the cutout of the Christmas tree off to one side. At the spring concert I held the cut out of flowers. Once, there weren't any cutouts to hold. The director took me aside. "I think it would really be best if you didn't sing," he said. "Would you please just mouth the words?"

Year after year I continued to pray for my miracle. "Please, Lord, just surround me with Your light, change me, and make me able to share your love with my voice," I would pray.

The day came when I graduated from high school and left my little town to go to college. My parents divorced soon after and both eventually left the area. I didn't return to that church until twenty-seven years later, when my husband and I along with Kile and Joel made a trip to that little town where I grew up.

We walked into the dimly lit church. I told them how I had hoped for a miracle, envisioned light beams coming down from heaven and me standing up in the congregation and singing with a beautiful voice.

They smiled because they knew that miracle had never happened. They had often heard me sing in my croaky, off-key voice. When I sang to them when they were babies, they cried. When I sang to them when they were little children, they put their hands over their ears and said, "Mommy, please don't sing!" When they stood beside me at church, they knew the embarrassment of having others turn to see where that awful noise was coming from.

What I have learned is that, although it did not happen in the way I had expected, my miracle really did occur, and that fact is the basis for my thanksgiving and praise.

The insight about my miracle came about some time after Terry had died. Unable to sleep, I curled up in my favorite chair in the family room to catch up on my journal. As I was writing about my grief, I realized that there had been a comforting presence with me through the fifteen months of Terry's illness. I laid down my pen and remembered those fifteen months with amazement. There had been ordeals that were unbearable. I had stood by his bedside and watched him die. How could I go on from there?

Looking back, I could see that the personal Jesus I have known for most of my life was there with me through it all. During that sleepless night I finally realized what it meant to have Christ in my life.

I tried to write my experiences in my journal, but the memories came faster than my pen could write. Finally, I simply put my journal aside and curled up tighter in the chair, hugging my bathrobe around me.

I thought about the good times in my life and how I had felt God's love during those times, how I had felt the presence of the living Lord, the Christ, walking with me. I also thought about the difficult times, and I remembered feeling His love for me then, too. Whatever the circumstances, His love was always there, surrounding me.

I pictured in my imagination God's love streaming down from heaven, enfolding me. I bolted upright in my chair! There before me was the picture of the miracle I had prayed for all those years! God's love had come to me, like a light from heaven. It had encompassed me, and it really HAD transformed me.

I remember my excitement at this new understanding. God had indeed answered my childhood prayers. He had, through His Son, come to me just as I'd asked. He had made a difference in my life. Maybe I still couldn't sing, but there were other ways I could praise Him.

I began to understand that I needed to share with others the difference His love had made in my life. I could write about what Jesus Christ had done and also share with people in my day-by-day life. I praise God that I got my miracle after all. I've learned that praise, either with or without music, is still praise. If my words can express God's love to someone else, I don't need to worry about the music. God will add the music to their lives. The most beautiful song of all is a song of praise, and I've learned that He gives each of us a unique and special way of singing it.

I think it is because of my remembering the long road between tragedy and joy, between heartbreak and healing, that makes me want to share this affirmation. When I see someone in despair, enduring the burdens of life, I want to say, "There is a loving God who sent His own Son to walk with us. You are not alone. You will get through this valley."

Those can be such empty, superficial-sounding words when we're in the midst of difficulties. What can I say? What can I do that will make a difference for that person who is hurting?

I look to the Scriptures for my answer. "So we are to use our different gifts in accordance with the grace God has given us. If our gift is to speak God's messages, we should do it according to the faith we have; if it is to serve, we should serve; if it is to teach, we should teach; if it is to encourage others, we should do so" (Romans 12:6–8).

This Scripture says to me that whatever way God has shown me to live within His will is the way I can share His love with others. By living within His will for me, I will be praising Him.

I think the way I live can provide the statement of praise I want to share. I hope that my life is an affirmation that God's love is real, that knowing Christ DOES make a difference in life. Then, I believe, I might be able to provide that spark of hope that someone might need. That is why I wrote this book.

Some time ago I received a letter from a mother whose son had just died. Once, years before, I had shared with her how God's assurances to me and my family after Terry's death helped us through that difficult time. I shared with her how we had learned to praise God again. She wrote to tell me that my words were helping her deal with her loss. I praise God for that.

We have choices in life. Even if we don't have choices in life's situations, we have choices in the way we will respond to them. Responding with praise to a God who can make a difference is a choice I am continuing to learn to make.

Yes, there are times when life hurts. Even so, joy can come into our lives. I thank God for that joy.

The psalmist of old knew about this. Psalm 40 says:

> I waited patiently for the Lord's help;
> then He listened to me and heard my cry.
> He pulled me out of a dangerous pit,
> out of the deadly quicksand.
> He set me safely on a rock and made me secure.
> He taught me to sing a new song,
> a song of praise to our God.
> Many who see this will take warning
> and will put their trust in the Lord. . . .
> I am surrounded by many troubles—too many to count!
> My sins have caught up with me, and I can no longer see;
> they are more than the hairs of my head,
> and I have lost my courage.
> Save me, Lord! Help me now! . . .
> May all who come to you be glad and joyful.
> May all who are thankful for your salvation
> always say, "How great is the Lord!"
> I am weak and poor, O Lord,

but you have not forgotten me.
You are my savior and my God—
hurry to my aid!

There was a time when I was in too much pain, was too beaten down to reach out to God with praise and thanksgiving. I think God understands that. I also think He waits patiently with us for that day when we are able to wish we had "a thousand tongues to sing our great Redeemer's praise."[1]
That day will come.
Yes, that day will come!

QUESTIONS FOR CONSIDERATION

1. What can you praise God for in your life?

2. How would you be different if you approached God with praise and thanksgiving?

3. Can you think of anyone you know whose life is an affirmation of praise to God?

4. What are some ways we can praise God in our lives?

5. What should we do if we do not feel that we can approach God with praise and thanksgiving?

Epilogue

Some years after Terry's death I wrote this in my journal:

Lord, it's been so many years since Terry died. What have we learned? How have we grown? What can we share with others?

There are days when I feel so strong. We have walked through the valley and here on the other side we find life abundant. We remember our son with grateful hearts for the ten years we did share.

There are other days, Lord, when I still feel such sadness at our loss, when I envy families who have never known this loss, when I feel resentment against people who don't seem to realize the blessing of their children. I am changed—not as quick to laugh, and I cannot bear to hear children crying.

Still, I know we have come a long way in these years. We've had several more moves, and have had to endure three more great heartaches, but we've also had the wonderful joy of a healthy new son born to us. I don't need to weep much any more. We've come a long way.

The sun is coming up as I write this, Lord. It is an affirmation, red and gold exclamation points across the sky! I guess that symbolizes what we've learned; that life is an affirmation of a loving God for us. As the sun rises we can still see a remainder of the night, of what has gone before; and each sunrise brings the promise of a new day, of what is yet to come. But the glory of the sunrise, whether there are clouds or not, is for right now.

For we have today.
TODAY!
I thank you for today, Lord.

While I wrote that a few years ago it is just as true for me today. There is a difference, though, in that I now find life even more richly abundant, and I find the living Lord walking beside me even more closely. I have learned to trust more, and hope more, and praise more.

Recently, when we lived in Jacksonville, Florida, my husband and I taught a Sunday school class for young adults. We are fortunate to be able to do the same here in Virginia. These classes so enrich our lives, perhaps because they are the age of our own adult children who live in another state. These young people fill an empty place in our lives. It is good for us to stay aware of the struggles of young adults today, of those difficult, life-affecting decisions with which they must deal. It is also good for us to focus on important lessons we have learned in order to share with them. One thing that I have told them over and over was that there are only two important things in life-our faith and our relationships. All else is really unimportant. Scripture tells us that. "Jesus answered, 'Love the Lord your God with all

Epilogue

your heart, with all your soul, and with all your mind. This is the greatest and most important commandment. The second most important commandment is like it: Love your neighbor as you love yourself. The whole Law of Moses and the teachings of the prophets depend on these two commandments" (Matthew 22: 37–40).

All of the lessons, which God has tried to teach me, fall into either one of those areas or the other. As I have been learning these lessons of life I feel as though I have been climbing up a mountain. It is not an easy thing to learn lessons. It is an uphill battle, but the higher we climb, the better our overview of life. The better our overviews of life, the more things are viewed in their right perspective.

I continue to believe that God gave us mountains as a visual aid for our lives. By learning those lessons of life that our loving Father would have us learn we climb higher and higher on our own personal mountain, bringing us up, out of ourselves, and closer to Him. We are able to get closer to Him, just as Jesus did during his time on earth.

Each time I make a trip to the mountains, I thank God for it: for the journey, for the view, for the vision. For each of us life's journey can become a special journey as we go to our own personal mountain.

I thank God for mountains.

Endnotes

CHAPTER TWO
1. "Dominion" by Jean Ingleow. *Bartlett's Familiar Quotations.* page 187. PermaBooks. New York. 1967.

CHAPTER THREE
1. "Awakenings". Producer—Lawrence Laker. Columbia Pictures. Screenplay by Steven Zaillian. Book by Oliver Sacks. Directed by Penny Marshall. 1990.
2. "Unanswered Prayer". Words and music by Larry B. Bastian, Pat Alger, and Garth Brooks. Copyright: Major Bob Music Company, Inc. (ASCAP)—Summer Music, Inc. (ASCAP). International copyright secured. Made in U.S.A. from *The Best of Garth Brooks.* page 54. Miami, FL CPP/Belen, Inc. 1992.

3. "Serenity Prayer" by Reinhold Niebuhr. From *The Power of Prayerful Living* by Doug Hill. page 156. Rodale Press. Emmaus, PA 2001.

CHAPTER FOUR

1. "As Comforting As An Arm Around My Shoulder" by Rosalie T. Turner, *Decision Magazine*. Minneapolis, MN April 1991. page 16–17.
2. "A Story From Weight Watchers®". From the *Clarion Ledger* newspaper. Jackson, MS section B. page 4. April 7, 1991.
3. "St. Francis of Assisi Prayer. *How To Pray For Inner Healing For Yourself and Others* by Rita Benet. page 45. Fleming H. Revell. Grand Rapids, MI 1984.

CHAPTER SIX

1. "Untitled"—by an anonymous Confederate soldier. From an insert in *Guidepost Magazine*. New York, NY 1985.

CHAPTER SEVEN

1. "How Great Thou Art". *The Book of Hymns*. page 17. The United Methodist Publishing House. Nashville, TN 1964/1966.

CHAPTER EIGHT

1. *The Blessing* by Gary Smalley and John Trent, Ph.D. page 118. Thomas Nelson Publishers, Nashville, TN 1986.
2. "Be Still My Soul". Arrangement of music copyright 1933 by Presbyterian Board of Christian Education. From *The Book of Hymns*. Page 209.

Endnotes

The United Methodist Publishing House. Nashille, TN 1964/1966.

CHAPTER NINE
1. "Trust and Obey". *The Book of Hymns.* Page 223. United Methodist Publishing House, Nashville, TN. 1964/1966.

CHAPTER TEN
1. "O For A Thousand Tongues To Sing". *The Book of Hymns,* page 1. The united Methodist Publishing House. Nashville, TN 1964/1966.

To order additional copies of

GOING
to the
MOUNTAIN

Please visit our web site at
www.pleasantword.com

Also available at:
www.amazon.com
and
www.barnesandnoble.com

CPSIA information can be obtained at www.ICGtesting.com
Printed in the USA
LVOW05s0853211113

362225LV00001B/4/P